NLP and Health

USING NLP TO ENHANCE YOUR HEALTH AND WELL-BEING

Ian McDermott
and Joseph O'Connor

Thorsons
An Imprint of HarperCollins*Publishers*

For Paulette

Thorsons
An Imprint of HarperCollins*Publishers*
77–85 Fulham Palace Road
Hammersmith, London W6 8JB
1160 Battery Street
San Francisco, California 94111–1213

Published by Thorsons 1996
10 9 8 7 6 5 4 3

A catalogue record for this book
is available from the British Library

ISBN 0 7225 3288 1

Printed and bound in Great Britain by
Creative Print and Design (Wales), Ebbw Vale

Contents

FOREWORD

The 'magic' of NeuroLinguistics has had much attention this past generation. This has had the effect of increasing the popular demand for learning and applying NLP principles in ever broader contexts.

In 17 years of using mind–body integration techniques in clinical medicine, I've witnessed many examples of 'proper-and-successful' as well as 'improper-and-unsuccessful' applications of such techniques and methods. However, I've also witnessed many instances of 'improper-and-successful' as well as 'proper-and-unsuccessful' applications of mind–body integration techniques – including what could be called formal NLP methods. This channel for success is therefore *not* via the formalistic, rigid application of 'Specific-Technique-X for Specific-Problem-X' – whether it is an NLP technique or otherwise.

The Primary Assumptions, or Presuppositions, of NLP are also its Guiding Principles. The 'principal-principle' is, indeed, *respect for the other person's model of the world!* Such presuppositions are as essential to the process of learning NLP as they are to the application of the discipline. The process simply cannot work if these principles are violated.

So, we recognize a number of guiding principles: that all behaviour has an underlying positive intention. That all techniques should serve to increase perceived choice. That there is no failure, only feedback. That people have all the ability they need to succeed. That the person with the greatest flexibility is the one who will most successfully navigate problem situations to achieve desired change. We also recognize that holding inflexibly to a preconceived notion of necessary technique will elicit resistance in a client/patient; it is a sign of lack of rapport. The problem, therefore, is not a client's resistance to change – rather, it is an inflexible communicator/practitioner. And since the meaning of the communication is the response one elicits, the practitioner must be ever-flexible in the interaction, in order to achieve in the patient the state of greater flexibility, greater perceived choice, greater learning opportunity and greater expression of one's own ability for achieving desired change.

OK – but so what?

Well, given that we already have within us all we need to succeed, then the application of mind–body integration methods such as NLP simply allows us to more readily access and harness our own abilities for change. If some principles and skills of NLP can be shared and taught in a clear and simple, 'de-mystified' manner, then an even greater contribution to humanity is made – for it allows more and more people to express these abilities, and thus to grow.

This is what Joseph O'Connor and Ian McDermott have accomplished in this book.

Through my association with Dr Deepak Chopra over the past two years (as the former Associate Medical Director of the Center for Mind Body Medicine, now the Chopra Center for Well-Being), I have had the great privilege of being the principal clinician in an environment of tremendous synthesis of many different healing traditions, disciplines and methods of spirit/mind/body integration.

Some time ago, I discovered that the NLP Presuppositions are consistent with principles of communicating and healing the mental and emotional Ama (toxins) within the Self written in the *Caraka Samhita*. This is the ancient Sanskrit text of Ayurveda, the Science of Life, which was written several thousand years ago! Although NLP may appear to be a 'new' discipline of barely 20 years age, its essence has been recognized and applied throughout the history of civilization. It has been a natural fit for me in adapting and integrating the principles and practice of NLP into the overall science and practice of Ayurveda and Mind–Body Medicine.

Many present-day practitioners of healing have found a comfortable balance of the NeuroLinguistic process of change within an overall paradigm of spiritual growth, transformation and evolution. In fact, it is precisely the 'Spirit' of the Presuppositions as guiding principles that creates the environment/state for change within which the specific techniques of NLP can have efficacy.

The authors understand this and communicate this clearly.

I am impressed with their ability to demystify – to reduce complex concepts into a framework of simplicity, while retaining the needed efficacy and clarity. Indeed, it is a mastery of the mystery.

I applaud their work.

The result is a well-written, easy-to-absorb guide to healing and change. It is a great asset for all of us – as practitioners of healing and as students of life.

I invite you to read on and enjoy!

Enrico Melson, MD
San Diego, California, USA
March 1996

Acknowledgements

Our thanks to all our teachers, and we want to give credit and recognition to John Grinder and Richard Bandler, co-developers of NLP, and to Robert Dilts for contributing so much to the field.

Many people helped us with this book. We would particularly like to thank Tim Hallbom, Suzi Smith and Janet Konefal for their help in making material available. Thank you to Dr Suzi Strang and Dr Jonas Miller, our medical proofreaders. Thank you to Hanne Lund for making her research on NLP and allergies available to us, and to Arron Williams for his help with the exercise and health sections.

We work together as equals, bringing our skills to this project and many others. Therefore the order in which the names appear on the cover of this book has no significance.

Ian McDermott and Joseph O'Connor
January 1996

INTRODUCTION

Is being healthy the same as not being ill? Surely there is more to health. For us, physical health is both a state and an ability – the energy and capacity to do what we care about and enjoy doing, and the ability to heal ourselves.

Health is paradoxical: you cannot directly 'will' yourself healthy, only watch as the body's marvellous healing ability comes into play naturally. However rich or poor, virtuous or cruel you may be seems to make little difference.

Health is positive. It does not mean giving up pleasures. It comes naturally from our lifestyle – relationships, diet, where and how we live. Health is not a possession, but a process. It is something we do and the result of how we think and feel. It is a state of being.

It is interesting that medical research is increasingly straying into fields that until now have been the province of the psychologist, and it is becoming difficult to draw the line between physical and mental factors in disease. To try to separate body and mind in health and illness is like trying to separate the salt from sea water with a knife. Mind and body are constantly influencing each other towards health or illness. Bodies do not get ill – people do.

This book is about health and healing, not about disease and curing. We want to complement the existing medical model, not try to supplant it or give an alternative. We want to explore how to enhance the incredible natural healing powers we all have – to reach the parts that standard medical science cannot reach.

Modern medicine excels in the treatment of medical and surgical emergencies, such as broken bones, bodily injuries, appendicitis and serious bacterial infections such as pneumonia that respond well to antibiotics. It can be truly life-saving. It also has good procedures for dealing with medical emergencies such as heart attacks, strokes and complications during childbirth. For the diseases and illnesses of modern living – allergies, hypertension, arthritis, asthma, cancer, osteoporosis, viral infections and nutritional disorders, however, modern medicine is far less confident.

We know a great deal about the mechanisms of illness but little about those of health. A dozen people may be equally exposed to infection, yet only two will become ill. Medicine can tell you in detail *how* they become ill, but why only those two? What protects the other 10? Likewise, two people may smoke heavily, eat badly and put in long hours at a stressful job, yet only one will become ill. Why? We are all constantly exposed to infectious micro-organisms, and no one escapes stress, sorrow and suffering. Yet illness is the exception, not the rule. We take our health for granted – until we become ill. Our immune system is constantly working to keep us well, just as our heart continues to beat and our lungs to take in air. Reduced immunity must be a critical component in every disease, otherwise we would forever be ill.

Health and illness are subjective experiences. We define them for ourselves, mostly from our feelings. There is no 'healthometer' that objectively measures health or 'dolorometer' that objectively measures pain. Neuro-Linguistic Programming (NLP) is the study of the structure of subjective experience – how we create our own unique internal world – so it is perfectly suited to exploring health.

The discipline of NLP grew up in the mid 1970s. At the heart of it is what is called 'modelling' – finding out how we do what we do. NLP models excellence in every field – health, sports, communication, teaching and learning, business and leadership, so that these skills may be taught to others. It models real people, not abstract ideals – what is possible and what has been done. The goal is excellence for all. In this book we are modelling health.

There is no universal diet, exercise regime or positive thinking method that works for everybody all the time. Needs vary, not just between people, but also for the same person over time. You will learn how to model your own states of excellence and enhance your health.

NLP has three main elements. The 'Neuro' refers to neurology, how mind and body are linked through the nervous system. The 'Linguistic' is about language – how we influence each other and ourselves through language. (The medical vocabulary of health and illness has built-in assumptions that direct our thoughts down well-trodden paths.) The 'Programming' is about repeated sequences of thought and behaviour – how we act to gain our goals and the consequences of our actions. The focus is on individual choice and ability.

Because NLP is such a broad discipline, this book is necessarily our own vision of applying NLP to health. It is a practical book. We are not aiming to teach NLP and you need know nothing about NLP or medicine to understand and use this book. NLP is not an alternative therapy, it is a body of ideas and a way of thinking. It is not about giving you the 'right' model of the world, but enriching the one you have. NLP is practical – you use it to make a difference and get what you want. The goal is being healthy.

There is a huge range of possible topics for a book on health, and we have selected those we think the most useful. Also, rather than cover all of NLP, we have looked at some of the main ways it can be used to enhance health and well-being. We have devoted a great deal of space to beliefs about health. They influence how we act, the sort of life we live, and enhance or block the effect of medical treatment. We have also dealt with three of the main challenges to health – stress, pain and ageing. The one message we want to impart in this book is that you *can* influence your physical health – your body is an integral part of you, not something that lets you down sometimes, and it has an amazing ability to learn and to heal.

So, how to begin your search for better health? There is no one answer, but we do have a story of Mullah Nasrudin, the Sufi holy man and jester.

Nasrudin would frequently ride across the border between Iran and Iraq on his horse. Each time he crossed, he would carry a bag of precious stones and a bag of medicinal potions, for which he had a legal customs trading permit. When the guard asked him his business, he would reply, 'I am a smuggler.'

The guard would search him each time and each time would find nothing unusual. Nasrudin became more and more prosperous on every trip and the guard became more and more suspicious, but he never found anything.

Eventually Nasrudin retired. The guard met him socially one day and asked, 'Nasrudin, now you have retired and cannot be prosecuted, please tell me what you were smuggling that we never found and that brought you these riches.'

'Horses,' replied Nasrudin.

A secret is best hidden in plain sight and can be found when you stop thinking it is hidden. We often look outside ourselves for answers that are within.

Your health is yours to create every day of your life. It is not found in drugs or dispensed by doctors, whatever their philosophy and methods of treatment, orthodox or unorthodox. Dazzled by the amazing new drugs and treatments that medicine develops, we forget that these are mostly heroic measures for disease already far advanced. Disease is a late signal that something is wrong and needs to be changed. For most of us, what we do right now is more important for our health. We will explore ways to change before disease insists.

We believe health is a way of being in the world and we offer this book as one part of a map to guide you towards it.

Your health is important. We wish to give you new ways to enhance it. We urge you to make full use of all health resources available to you – and that includes your doctor. We wish to stress that this book is not a substitute for the advice and treatment of a physician or other health professional.

I

HEALTH, MEDICINE AND LOGICAL LEVELS

> To administer medicines to diseases that have already devel-
> oped and to suppress revolts which have already developed is
> comparable to the behaviour of those persons who begin to dig
> a well after they have become thirsty, and of those who begin to
> cast weapons after they have already engaged in battle. Would
> these actions not be too late?
>
> *The Yellow Emperor's Classic of Internal Medicine*, 200 BC

What does *being healthy* mean to you?
How would you define being healthy?
How does it feel?
What are you able to do?
How do you know when you are healthy?

These are questions about your individual definition of health.
We hope you will live it more fully in the course of this book.
We deliberately asked you about 'being healthy', not about
'health'. Being healthy is something you are actively engaged in –
something you *do*. 'Health' is a noun, a static concept. There is a
difference. Check for yourself in your own experience – think
of 'being healthy'. If you have a mental picture of being healthy,
it will probably involve a sense of movement. In contrast, a picture
of 'health' is likely to be like a still photograph. This is an
example of NLP – how the words we use change our subjective
experience.

Could this make a difference? Definitely. A static picture of
health might seem something separate to be grasped sometime in
the future, rather than something you are living now. While we
will use both expressions in this book, think of health as a process
– something you are creating.

KEEPING YOUR BALANCE

When you are healthy you are able to conduct your life how you want – individually, emotionally, socially and spiritually. Being healthy implies you have goals. Illness and disease mean you lose the freedom to pursue those goals. We also think being healthy is a state of balance for body, mind and spirit, a natural state of being ourselves. Each of us is unique and so is our state of balance. There is no 'health prescription' that satisfies everybody. This balance is like that of an athlete walking along a beam – moving and fluid. Small readjustments are needed all the time – shifting your body this way and that, continually swaying to keep your balance. A sudden gust of wind might disturb your balance. You sway for a moment, then your natural healing abilities bring you back into balance. Perhaps you have been walking 'too close to the edge'. The stiffer and more rigid you are, the more likely you are to fall.

There is no monolithic state of health, as opposed to illness. Our bodies readjust all the time to the changing circumstances. No one completely escapes illness, loss, sorrow and worry. We deal with the 'slings and arrows of outrageous fortune' as best we can. Our bodies have tremendous innate healing abilities – which we often ignore in favour of a helping hand from the medicine cabinet. Sometimes we also need outside help in the form of medical treatment to augment our natural healing process and bring us back to balance.

Sickness can be divided into illness and disease. Disease is a demonstrable pathological process. Illness is a subjective experience, a feeling that all is not well. We feel illness in the body but it affects every part of our lives – our work, our relationships with others and how we feel about ourselves. We may feel ill for no apparent reason, a doctor may find nothing 'wrong' with us, there is no disease, but the feeling of malaise is very real.

Modern medicine tends to treat all illness as disease. From the point of view of healing, disease is a special case of illness that may need professional medical treatment. Disease is when we have lost our balance and need outside help to regain it. Diseases are not cured without mobilizing our own powers of healing.

Most illnesses are self-limiting – some research puts the figure as high as 80 per cent[1] – that is, you heal yourself regardless of medical intervention.

1   Inglefinger, F., 'Health: a matter of statistics or feeling?', *New England Journal of Medicine* 296 (1977), 448–9

In many of the remaining cases, medical treatment will be successful – often dramatically so. However, in some cases, wrong diagnosis, inadequate treatment, damaging side-effects from drugs or complications from surgery may result in iatrogenic problems for some patients – that is, problems caused by the treatment.

THREE THOUSAND YEARS OF MEDICINE

Nearly 2,500 years ago, Hippocrates taught that being healthy was evidence that an individual had achieved a state of harmony both within themselves and within their environment, and that whatever affects the mind affects the body. Now, we seem to be coming back to this point of view. As Mark Twain said, 'The ancients steal all our best ideas.'

This insight was lost in the seventeenth century when Western scientific thinking, led by Descartes, divided human beings into separate domains: a body (soma) and a mind (psyche). Two different words were mistaken for two separate things, leading to a dualistic way of thinking and a medicine that was dominated by the body. Psychological influences on the body were not a legitimate scientific study until well into the twentieth century. Somehow the body was taken to be 'real' in a way that the mind was not, so thoughts became 'unreal'. Anything that did not have a solidly visible physiological base was 'all in the mind'. Subjective experience was discounted. A patient was a body to be cured, and medicine concentrated largely on treating disease and illness as deviations from a biological norm, using physical interventions to compensate for any imbalances. The human athlete gracefully walking on the beam was replaced by a robot.

The period from 1780 to 1850 was known as 'the age of heroic medicine' (certainly you had to be a hero to withstand the treatments). Bleeding was the commonest method of treatment for a variety of ailments – usually a pint at a time. Another popular treatment was intestinal purging, often induced by calomel (mercurous chloride), so mercury poisoning was common. Such heroic treatments must have hastened many patients to their deaths.

In 1803 a German pharmacist isolated morphine from opium. Towards the end of the nineteenth century heroic methods of treatment were replaced by the use of large quantities of morphine and cocaine for many illnesses. Heroin was synthesized in 1898 and enthusiastically marketed for a short time as a safe and effective cough medicine.

Since the 1870s medicine has made great advances against a whole range of infectious diseases through understanding the role of micro-organisms in causing disease. In 1882 Robert Koch isolated the tubercle bacillus. Louis Pasteur had already demonstrated that it was possible to immunize against diseases. Diseases that had killed millions, such as tuberculosis, diphtheria and smallpox, could now be prevented.

Throughout the twentieth century more effective drugs have been found. Antibiotics were discovered in the 1940s and now we can routinely cure many diseases that were hitherto fatal. However, medical research still seeks to progress by the same methods that worked in the past. A huge industry is now committed to developing drugs to every ailment.

THE LIMITS OF MEDICINE

Medical science has limits and we discover them soon enough when we, or someone we care about, are ill or in pain. Better treatment does not mean better health. Medical care improves, but rates of illness continue to rise. Most suffering is beyond the reach of medicine.

There are three main ways of measuring the general health of the population. First, whether you live at all – infant mortality. Secondly, how well you live. This can be roughly measured by work days lost through sickness. Thirdly, how long you live – adult mortality and average lifespan. The effect of modern medical practice, systems of prescribing and hospitalization influence these standard indices by less than 10 per cent. The rest are governed by factors over which doctors have little or no control – amount of exercise, social conditions, eating habits, air quality – in other words social and environmental conditions and individual lifestyle.

We would not wish to demean biomedical achievements. Within their chosen area of treating disease their impact has been considerable, increasing both longevity and quality of life. However, the greatest advances in public health have been achieved through sewage disposal, water purification, pasteurizing milk and better nutrition. It is these that have led to the greatest increase in quality and length of life.

In 1900 the average American life expectancy from birth was about 48 years. In 1990 it was 79. However, most of this increase has been because medicine has been successful at reducing infant mortality by preventing and treating dangerous diseases of childhood. Life expectancy has not increased very much for adults. At the moment, a 45-year-old man in good health can expect to live roughly another 29 years. In 1900 a man of 45 could expect to live about another 25 years. We are healthier today not so much because we are receiving better treatment when we are ill, but because we tend not to become ill in the first place. The main effect of many medical advances is that people are now able to live longer *with their illnesses.*

Modern medicine acts as if all health problems are biological and can ultimately be solved through research. But the diseases that threaten us now are very different from those infectious diseases against which medicine has proved so successful. Now the main threats are degenerative diseases such as heart disease, cancer, rheumatoid arthritis, osteoporosis and diabetes, and those associated with a breakdown of the immune system, such as AIDS. Alzheimer's disease is an enormous problem as the population lives longer. A number of new illnesses are coming to light – myalgic encephalomyelitis (ME), seasonal affective disorder (SAD) and repetitive strain injury (RSI). Many environmental factors are now seen as contributing to disease – and air pollution and overcrowding cannot be immunized against or easily prescribed for.

Nature also keeps pace with our medical ingenuity. As fast as we develop drugs to cure infections, the micro-organisms change and adapt. For example, pneumonococcus is a bacterium responsible for meningitis, pneumonia and middle ear infections. Research at the American Centre for Disease Control and Prevention in 1995[2] found that 25 per cent of patients were infected by a strain of pneumonococcus that was resistant to penicillin. Ten years earlier, in 1985 the frequency of penicillin-resistant pneumonococcus was less than $1/10$ of 1 per cent.

A survey of half of the intensive care units in Europe carried out by the *Journal of the American Medical Association* found more than 20 per cent of the patients they examined had infections which were acquired in the unit. These infections were resistant to antibiotics. A three-week stay in intensive care increases your risk of

2 *North Eastern Journal of Medicine,* 24 August 1995

infection 33 times. As fast as we find drugs, micro-organisms become resistant to them.

Medicine has less impact on our health than we think and we have more influence than we give ourselves credit for. This is clear when doctors are not available. In 1973, when doctors in Israel were on strike for a month, admissions to hospital went down by 85 per cent. The death rate dropped by 50 per cent to reach its lowest recorded level. The previous low level was 20 years before – also during a doctors' strike. During a doctors' strike in Los Angeles County in 1976 to protest against high malpractice insurance premiums, the death rate fell by nearly 20 per cent. Sixty per cent fewer operations were performed. At the end of the strike the death rate quickly rose to normal levels. Such strikes bring home that your *individual* longevity and *individual* health are your responsibility.

RESPONSIBLE OR BLAMEWORTHY?

Does this mean we are somehow to blame for being ill? *Absolutely not.* Illness and disease are hard enough to bear without the extra feeling of guilt that somehow you brought it on yourself.

First we would like to make a distinction between staying healthy and curing yourself of disease. Disease is a late sign that something is wrong and demands action. Some extreme forms of holistic medicine claim that you should be able to cure yourself without medical treatment and if you fail, you did not try hard enough. Some unorthodox cancer therapies adopt this view too. The idea that you brought the disease on yourself without the help of doctors and really ought to be able to get rid of it without their help either is unreasonable. A life-threatening disease has a long and complex build up; there is no simple cause. Health and disease are not wholly in the body or in the mind, they are in both. Any disease, especially a serious disease like cancer, shows that the body is a long way out of balance and you need to take all necessary and appropriate steps to bring it back into balance. And when you overbalance there is a critical point when you cannot get back by yourself. You need all the help you can get – for both body and mind.

Some people may blame themselves for their illness because it is preferable to feeling helpless, a dreadful feeling that saps our strength, our spirit and our immune system. They then seek to fight the disease and the feeling of helplessness with will-power alone. But we are not helpless; we have many resources that can help us. Just as disease is a combination of factors, many outside our control, so is the cure. It is just as unbalanced to feel completely responsible for your own health as it is to delegate responsibility to the medical profession and make no effort of your own. Blaming yourself makes it more difficult to heal yourself.

So to say we cause our own sickness and thus are responsible for curing it is too simplistic. If you lie out in the sun without protection for a long time you will get sunburned. If you walk in front of a moving car you will be badly hurt. These are simple, obvious relationships, easily seen because effect follows cause immediately. But cause and effect do not work so directly over time in something as complex and beautiful as the human body.

Health issues are complicated because the body is a complex living system. All parts can and do affect all other parts. What you can do is take control of what is within your power. There is abundant statistical evidence to link smoking with ischaemic heart disease, emphysema and lung cancer, for example. However, no one can say that if you smoke they will definitely happen to you. It is equally mistaken to conclude smoking is harmless because you have a friend in his eighties who smokes a packet of cigarettes a day and can run a marathon. Smoking is a habit that is under your control and it increases the odds of serious disease. If you would not gamble money on the odds in a casino, it makes no sense to gamble your health on them either.

Connections are also difficult to see because medical knowledge advances slowly. It can take many years before illness can be linked to an event in the past. It was decades before we recognized that asbestos was carcinogenic. We are presently discovering a link between sunburn and skin cancer and we now shudder when we read of servicemen watching the first atom bomb tests from just a few miles away. We must simply act as best we can given our state of knowledge at any time.

In this book we will be looking particularly at ways of thinking and being that will move ourselves towards health and away from illness. We have many resources we can use to become and stay healthy; modern medicine is only one of them. What is important is your own commitment to your own health.

LEVELS OF HEALTH

Your health is your total way of being and is influenced by many factors – individual, psychological, social, physical and nutritional. There are two important questions about any health issue:

What factors can you influence?
Which will bring about the most change?

Some factors we can influence a great deal, others only partially or not at all. NLP has developed a useful way of thinking about different levels of control and influence that is particularly useful in the field of health. They are called 'neurological levels' or just 'logical levels'. The concept has been developed primarily by Robert Dilts.

The first level is the *environment* – your surroundings and the people you are with. Environmental factors like the quality of the air we breathe and the food we eat are very important to our health. Drugs, the main medical intervention, are also on this environmental level.

We can make a distinction between internal and external environment. What are you putting into your internal environment? What quality of air, what quality of food? For example, we may eat plenty of fruit to make sure of the recommended daily allowance of vitamins, but not only may they have taken so long to reach the shops that the vitamin content has deteriorated, but they may also contain high quantities of pesticides from modern farming methods. An external environmental factor that may pose a hazard is the high levels of electromagnetic radiation from electric power lines. This has been linked in several studies to increased risk of childhood cancers.[3]

The social environment is particularly important. There have been numerous animal studies where increasing the size of the group while keeping all other aspects of the environment constant has led to a rise in infant mortality, an increase in arteriosclerosis and a reduced resistance to disease.[4] Much social planning seems

3 *Lancet*, 20 November 1993

4 Calhoun, J., 'Population density and social pathology', *Scientific American* 206 (1962), 139–48

to be running the same experiment with humans, with results that we are just beginning to discover.

Problems of overcrowding, food production methods and air quality are not under most people's control. Changing these environmental factors takes time and persistent political action. In the meantime, short of living on a remote island and growing your own food, you have to deal with the environment as best you can.

Other people – friends, family and work colleagues – are also part of our environment, and a huge amount of evidence has built up since 1980 that the quality of our relationships has an enormous impact on health. In some studies it overshadows all other variables such as where you live and how well off you are. Loneliness, isolation and poor interpersonal relationships are a significant health hazard.

The second level is *behaviour*. Behaviour is what we do. There are two health aspects to this – avoiding unhealthy habits and cultivating healthy ones.

This brings us to the third level – what NLP calls *capability*. Capability is repeated, consistent actions and habits. For example, one cigarette is unlikely to do any harm, but a smoking habit is associated with an increased risk of lung and heart disease. Diet is another example. The occasional cream cake, biscuit and canned drink does not hurt, but a continuous diet of these leads to an increased risk of obesity, diabetes and dental decay. Habits are not stopped by will-power but usually by finding the goal behind the habit and working for that in a healthier way.

This is also the level of what NLP calls 'strategies' – habitual ways of thinking and responding. We have strategies for dealing with stress, forming relationships, becoming angry, what and when we eat, and when and how much we exercise. Strategies are thought sequences that we use consistently and therefore lead to habitual actions. There is evidence from behavioural medicine that states of mind such as depression and pessimism are associated with definite health problems. These are the results of habitual ways of thinking. We will explore this in Chapter 8.

When NLP developed, in the mid 1970s, there was a gap in psychological thinking. The Behaviourist psychology of the time was about action and reaction, stimulus–response, the interaction between environment and behaviour. There were also many value-based psychological systems, stressing the power of beliefs, values and self-esteem. All these are valuable, but the practical how-tos were conspicuously missing. NLP fills this gap with the capability level. Modelling success, it gives techniques and tools; analysing the structure of our experience, it makes healthy strategies understandable and possible for all.

The fourth level is *beliefs and values*. They have enormous influence on our health. Beliefs are the principles that guide our actions. They determine how we view ourselves, how we react to others and what meaning we make of our experiences. The placebo response shows that we can heal ourselves if we believe in the efficacy of the medicine, regardless of whether the medicine has any physiological effect or not. Something that we think of as purely mental (a belief) has an effect on the body that is real and tangible. Also, research in behavioural medicine is finding that the degree to which we believe we have control over our reactions is an important protection against the unhealthy effects of stress.

We often operate on the principle of 'seeing is believing'. But unfortunately, by the time you see the result of an unhealthy habit, it is too late – you are ill. The evidence you need for the belief is the thing you want to avoid.

Beliefs also have a more pervasive effect. For example, if you believe that there is a drug for every ailment, you will probably behave differently from someone who believes that their health is predetermined by hereditary. We will explore the effects of beliefs on health in detail in Chapter 4.

Values are what are important to us, those things we pursue – health, wealth, happiness, safety, love. Values act as magnets for our behaviour. Why do we do what we do? To gain what is important to us and avoid those things that are hurtful. So behavioural medicine often has no impact because it does not take the level of beliefs and values into account. People will not change unless they believe there is good reason to do so and it gains them something of importance or moves them away from something they want to avoid. Beliefs and values are not logical (although they are not necessarily illogical) – you cannot usually argue someone out them, although beliefs do shift over time. (Not many adults believe in Father Christmas.)

The fifth level is *identity*. Identity is your sense of yourself, the central beliefs and values that define you and your mission in life, in your own eyes. If someone has a chronic illness, they may adopt the identity of 'a patient'. This hampers recovery. A patient is a person who is ill. As long as they think of themselves as a patient, they are still ill. A person is neither their illness nor their pain, though both may be overwhelming at times. On the other hand, 'I am a healthy person' is an identity statement that can have a tremendous impact on your health.

Finally, the sixth level is *beyond identity*, or the spiritual level – your connection to others and to that which is more than your identity, however you choose to think of it.

To summarize:

Health affects every neurological level and is affected by every level. It is multi-dimensional. Your health involves all of you – environment, behaviour, thoughts, beliefs, identity and beyond.
NLP defines the levels. It gives us practical methods so we can:

work on the environmental level by building and maintaining strong relationships.

work on the levels of behaviour and capability by forming healthy habits and thinking strategies, allowing us to respond more resourcefully. So we experience less stress and are more in control.

work on the level of beliefs and values by becoming aware of our beliefs and what is important to us. NLP gives specific ways for us to resolve conflicting beliefs and to change old beliefs for ones that support our health more fully.

work on the identity and spiritual levels by aligning all the other levels.

FINDING THE RIGHT LEVEL

Neurological levels are very useful in defining health issues. First define the level you are dealing with. Some health problems are environmental, for example poor air quality and unpleasant working conditions. There is even a 'sick building syndrome' that is recognized by the World Health Organization. The symptoms can include fatigue, headaches, skin reactions, dry throat and sore eyes. There is no one cause for the syndrome, but people working in air-conditioned offices seem to be more susceptible.

Our own experience tells us that natural surroundings are pleasant and relaxing. We seek them out in our holidays. There is something satisfying about watching the flow of water in a stream, ceaselessly moving in chaotic patterns, yet with an overall flow and direction. Medical research backs up what our bodies intuitively know: pleasant surroundings speed recovery from illness. We may not know our blood pressure is going down when we sit and watch nature, but we feel it in our bodies.

A ROOM WITH A VIEW

Roger Ulrich[5] at the Department of Geography, University of Delaware, has done an interesting study on the effect of the environment on 46 hospital patients, all of whom were recovering from gall bladder surgery. Half the patients were in hospital rooms with a view of a brown brick wall. The other half had a room with a view that overlooked a row of trees with foliage. Those who had the view of nature spent significantly less time in hospital after their surgery (they went home on average a day and a half earlier than the other group) and needed fewer doses of painkilling medication. They also had slightly fewer post-operative complications.

A view of a brick wall from a hospital bed is not as pleasant as a view of trees and Ulrich's research suggests it can hamper recovery. When our copy-editor read this, she told us of her own experience in hospital. She smashed her elbow in a hockey match and found herself recovering in a ward with a view of a wall. She shared

5   Ulrich, R., 'View through a window may influence recovery from surgery', *Science* 224, 27 April 1984, 420–1

the ward with many seriously ill 70-year-old patients. Although a supposedly fit and otherwise healthy 21 year old, she was the one who always asked for painkillers. She also suffered post-operative complications: her arm rejected the metal pin and the whole area went septic under the cast. It did not mend properly and she could not straighten her elbow for months.

Many intensive care units (ICUs) have no windows at all and some patients suffer from a condition known as 'ICU delirium', consisting of hallucinations, disorientation and memory loss. It significantly delays their recovery. ICU delirium is twice as frequent in patients in rooms that have no windows.[6] Also, patients in ICU rooms without windows suffer three times the rate of serious depression. Sick buildings can produce sick people.

To be healthy, the physical body needs an adequate diet, a certain amount of exercise, sufficient and regular sleep, clean air and a level of comfort and safety. These are basic requirements and no amount of mental effort will change them. Start by changing your physical environment if it is not a healthy one.

Health problems can occur at any level and need to be addressed at the right level. For example, a doctor who was on our NLP training confessed that when people used to come to him complaining that they did not know how to relax, he used to suggest that they go on holiday. On learning about logical levels, he realized that this was an environmental prescription and unlikely to change the patient's situation, except perhaps in the short term. The holiday would be relaxing, but would not address the complaint at the capability level – *how* to relax.

Changing habits is not straightforward even when the health benefits are obvious. We act in our best interests – as we perceive them. Beliefs and values are some of the strongest filters. A person may know what to do (behaviour) and even how to do it (capability), but still not do it because it is not important to him (values) or he believes it will make no difference (beliefs).

Beliefs determine what we do with the doctor's prescriptions. Many are untouched because the patient found visiting the doctor was reassuring in itself. There is an apocryphal story of a patient taking part in a double blind drug trial who asked his doctor whether his last medication was different from the others.

6   Wilson, L., 'Intensive care delirium: the effect of outside deprivation in a windowless unit', *Archives of Internal Medicine* 130 (1972), 225–6

'Why do you ask?' replied the doctor, trying to appear non-committal, for in a double blind trial, neither doctor nor patient knows which is the 'real' drug and which is the placebo.

'Well,' replied the patient, 'last week the drugs you gave me floated when I flushed them down the toilet. This week, they sank.'

It is important not to take comments and criticism of behaviour and capability at an identity level. Criticism of what you do is not criticism of *you*. Blame and criticism can be very hurtful and lead to rumination, recrimination and depression, all of which may weaken your immune system.

Many people have their identity invested in their job. When asked 'What do you do?', they reply with their job description. So it is no wonder that unemployment, redundancy and even retirement are experienced by many as a rejection. Losing a job is like a bereavement for many people – they feel they have lost part of themselves. They become depressed and lose their spirit for life and may become ill.

This tendency to confuse behaviour with identity starts in childhood. Adults will say something like '*You* are very bad' when a child misbehaves. Children are very trusting, they believe what adults say and the foundation for confusing identity with behaviour is built early in life.

One of the most important ways to reduce health-threatening stress is to make a clear distinction between what you do and who you are.

CULTURAL IDENTITY

We also define our identity by race and culture. Doctor Leonard Syme, an epidemiologist working in the School of Public Health at the University of California, Berkeley, has made a detailed study over many years of Japanese immigrants to the United States.[7] The Japanese have one of the highest life expectancies and lowest rates of heart disease of nations that keep health statistics. Yet Japan is not a pastoral paradise. It is an advanced industrialized nation, with a particularly bad air pollution problem and a fast pace of life.

7   Syme, L., *People Need People*, Institute for the Study of Human Knowledge, 1982

The Japanese could enjoy a very favourable genetic inheritance, or their diet could protect them from heart disease. However, within a generation, Japanese immigrants to the United States who adopt a typical Western diet high in fat and cholesterol become as vulnerable to heart disease as their hosts – except for those Japanese who keep close ties with Japanese values and community, and continue to use their own language. This is true even for those who eat a typical American diet.

The Japanese have a value they call *amae* – a belief that a person's well-being depends on co-operation and goodwill in their group. Being part of a group and sharing basic values seems to offer some protection against degenerative illnesses that are linked to diet. No other variables such as age, sex, social class or other health habits explained this effect. Heart disease is tangible, identity is intangible, yet the two interact. One of the problems of medicine is finding scientifically valid ways of measuring this connection.

LANGUAGE AND LEVELS

The language a person uses shows what level they are coming from. Here are some examples:

Identity	'I am a smoker.'
Belief	'Smoking is bad for you.'
Capability	'I learnt how to inhale when I was 13.'
Behaviour	'I smoke 20 cigarettes a day.'
Environment	'Many of my friends smoke too.'

Identity	'I am a healthy person.'
Belief	'Being healthy means I enjoy life more.'
Capability	'I keep healthy by running three miles every week.'
Behaviour	'I went to the gym for a workout on Wednesday.'
Environment	'I have made many friends at the gym.'

Identity	'I am a cancer survivor.'
Belief	'Cancer can be cured.'
Capability	'I coped well with the chemotherapy treatment.'
Behaviour	'I am seeing the doctor tomorrow for a check up.'
Environment	'I have found the local cancer support group really helpful.'

Identity	'I am a naturally calm person.'
Belief	'Staying calm under pressure helps me work better.'
Capability	'I practise relaxation exercises every day.'
Behaviour	'When my supervisor shouted at me, I took a deep breath and counted to 10.'
Environment	'I like to go to the park at lunchtime to relax.'

Identity	'I am not the sort of person who gains weight easily.'
Belief	'I will achieve my target weight.'
Capability	'I can eat what I like because I never put on weight.'
Behaviour	'I ate a bar of chocolate after dinner yesterday.'
Environment	'The food in that local French restaurant is so good, I always have second helpings.'

Neurological levels are not a hierarchy, more of a circle or a hologram. Each level affects the others and all are important for health. A good environment, with good friends, is important, but not necessarily sufficient if you have a belief you are unhealthy. And a person with such a belief may not bother to give themselves a healthy environment anyway. You can impact your health not only by changing your environment, but also by working on your beliefs. Health is both physical and mental, and the effects of each cross the boundary into the other.

Beliefs govern much of your behaviour, so the most effective way to change behaviour is often to change beliefs. Often trying to change your behaviour becomes a matter of will-power and it is all too easy to slip back into the status quo. We are all familiar with the 'New Year's resolution' effect – all those good resolutions which scarcely last to the end of January. Changing habits is easier when you realize that they are no longer part of your self-image. You just outgrow them effortlessly. This is when the change in behaviour is backed by a change in beliefs and values, and a more complete sense of self.

When you think of your own health goal or are confronted with a health problem, identify which level it is on:

• You may need more information from the environment. If so, do nothing until you have found out what you need to know.
• You may have all the information, but not know exactly what to do.
• You may know what to do, but not know how to do it.
• You may wonder whether you can do it, whether it is worth it and in keeping with your beliefs and values.
• You may wonder 'Is it really me?'

THE PHYSIOLOGY OF NEUROLOGICAL LEVELS

Neurological levels have broad physiological counterparts. The deeper the level, the more neurology is involved. We react to our environment with the peripheral nervous system. Behaviour and capabilities involve the motor and cortical layers of the nervous system – our conscious and semi-conscious actions. Beliefs and values mobilize our autonomic nervous system – the part that regulates the internal states of your body such as your heart rate, blood pressure and digestion. When you are arguing for your beliefs and values your breathing rate changes and your pulse quickens. The identity level corresponds to your immune system – that part of you that protects you from disease by distinguishing between self and 'foreign' bodies. And beyond identity? We do not really know. It may involve a balance in the autonomic nervous system between the sympathetic branch, which energizes and increases your heart rate, respiration and blood pressure, and the parasympathetic branch, which calms them.

Logical levels demonstrate the three parts of NLP: Neurology, for each level brings in more of our neurology into play; Linguistic, as each level is shown by the language we use;

Programming because we take different actions depending on the level we want to influence.

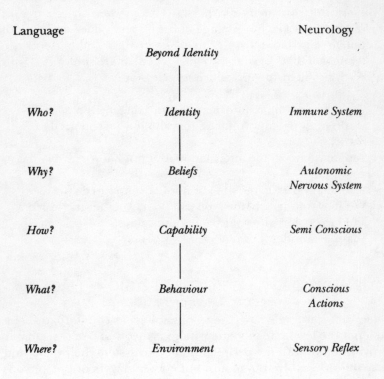

Language		Neurology
	Beyond Identity	
Who?	Identity	Immune System
Why?	Beliefs	Autonomic Nervous System
How?	Capability	Semi Conscious
What?	Behaviour	Conscious Actions
Where?	Environment	Sensory Reflex

Logical levels of health

ALIGNING YOUR HEALTH

Here is a practical exercise to explore these levels in your own health.

First, remember a time when you felt really healthy.
With that in mind, take your time to think about these questions.

Environment

Where were you?
What people were around you at the time?
What were your surroundings like?
What time of the year was it?
Is there a particular time of the day when you feel really healthy?
What relationships were important to you then?

Behaviour

What were you doing?

Capability

What skills did you have then?
What did you feel capable of?
What was the quality of your thinking?

Beliefs and Values

What did you believe about your health?
Was it a natural state?
Was it easy or difficult to achieve?
Why did you want to be healthy?
What did it get for you?
What was important to you about being healthy?
What might have stopped you from being healthy?

Identity

What is it like to be a healthy person?
What is your mission in life?
How does being a healthy person help you to achieve this mission?
How does being healthy add to your sense of self?

Beyond Identity

Think about how you are connected to all other living beings and whatever you believe is beyond yourself. For some people this is the religious or spiritual realm. How does being healthy connect you to others and help you go beyond yourself?

FOOD FOR THOUGHT

Disease: A definite morbid process having a characteristic train of symptoms; it may affect the whole body or any of its parts, and its aetiology, pathology and prognoses may be known or unknown.

Dorland's Illustrated Medical Dictionary, 26th edition, 1981

The body is a machine, so built and composed of nerves, muscles, veins, blood and skin, that though there were no mind in it at all, it would not cease to have the same functions.

René Descartes, *Traite de L'homme*

Theoretically, every disease is psychosomatic, since emotional factors influence all body processes through nervous and humoral pathways.

Franz Alexander, *Psychosomatic Medicine: Its principles and applications*
(Norton, 1950)

In 90% of patients seen by a general practitioner, the effects of the treatment are unknown or there is no specific remedy that influences the course of the illness.

Sir George Pickering, 'Therapeutics: Art or science?'
Journal of the American Medical Association 242 (1979), 649–53

Le germe n'est rien, c'est le terrain qui est tout.
(The microbe is nothing, the context is everything.)

Louis Pasteur – the French chemist and bacteriologist who
developed the germ theory of disease – and who on his
deathbed asserted the importance not of the microbe but of its
host environment

The twentieth century will be remembered chiefly not as an age of political conflicts and technical inventions but as an age in which society dared to think of the health of the whole human race as a practical objective.

Arnold Toynbee

2

THE FOUR PILLARS OF HEALTH

NLP began by modelling excellent communication skills – how fine communicators used language to forge good relationships and achieve their goals. Communication skills are usually taken to mean communicating with others, but in the area of health how you communicate with yourself is just as important.

NLP is built on four simple principles which in our view constitute four pillars of health. The first is the quality of our relationships. Good relationships are crucial to good health. Our friends and loved ones are part of us, they affirm our identity. Quality is more important here than quantity. To be able to share your thoughts and feelings with one or two close friends is usually better than having a host of more superficial relationships. For this we need to build and maintain rapport. Rapport is the quality of relationship built on trust. When you have rapport you influence others and are open to influence.

There is abundant evidence that individuals with close supportive relationships and a strong social network are ill less often, recover more quickly and have a lower death rate. There are many reasons why. Good friends cannot be collected over the counter at the chemist, but they support you in health and help you recover in a way that drugs cannot. Friends and family encourage you to look after yourself and will help you when you are ill. It is devastating to feel lonely, that no one cares. It saps the will to recover.

The effect of social ties on health was clearly shown in the 1979 study by Berkman and Syme in Almeda County, California.[1] The

---

1 Berkman, L., and Syme, S., 'Social networks, host resistance and mortality: a nine year follow-up study of Almeda County residents', *American Journal of Epidemiology* 109 (1979), 186–204

study covered nine years. A simple index of social ties was made for each resident involving the number of close friends and relatives they had, whether or not they were married, and attendance in formal and informal groups. Those with few ties had mortality rates that were two to five times higher than the others. This was independent of other risk factors such as drinking, smoking, exercise and obesity. The link held for both sexes across every socio-economic group. People who have a good network of supportive friends in whom they can confide also tend to be more generally healthy. Having good friends is a good predictor of both health and longevity.[2]

Another research study at the New Mexico School of Medicine found that individuals who had at least one person they could confide in had significantly higher markers of immune functioning and lower levels of substances such as serum cholesterol that are strongly associated with increased risk of heart disease.[3]

RAPPORT WITH YOURSELF

What of your relationship with yourself? You are the one person you always have to confide in. What is it like living with yourself? For many it is like living with several different people all wanting different things. They bargain, threaten and cajole as well as support each other. How well do these different parts of you get on?

Rapport with yourself can be on several levels. Firstly, there is rapport with your physical body. How at home do you feel in your body? Do you like it? Does it seem like an enemy sometimes, turning against you and falling ill? How well do you know it? We are often preoccupied with our bodies, yet unaware of how they work. We tend to ignore them when they work well and curse them when they do not. Not very friendly. We neglect to pay attention to the messages they give us. What is your body telling you right at

2   House, J., Landis, K., and Umberson, D., 'Social relationships and health', *Science* 241 (1988), 540–5

3   Thomas, P. D., Goodwin, J. M., and Goodwin, J. S., 'Effect of social support on stress-related changes in cholesterol level, uric acid level and immune function in an elderly sample', *American Journal of Psychiatry* 142 (6) (1985), 735–7

this moment about your physical comfort, your alertness and your digestion?

Secondly, there is the rapport between those different parts of your mind. Minds do not really have 'parts', it is just a useful way of talking. You have probably been in a situation where you were torn between several courses of action or wanted two incompatible things at once, for example to stay home and to go out, or to take this work or that work. Rapport here means being able to reconcile potentially conflicting wishes in such a way that over time, all are honoured. You may have to negotiate between two parts of your mind, just as you would between two people. Mental rapport is when these different parts of you work in harmony. They may be playing different instruments, but they both have the same score and you are the conductor.

Thirdly, there is rapport between body and mind. Does your body protest at some of the work you tell it to do? Body and mind are different aspects of the same being – a human being. Health comes from both working together. Our thoughts have real physical effects and our body affects our thoughts – imagine trying to make important decisions when you have 'flu.

Lastly, there is the dimension of rapport at a spiritual level. This can be about a sense of belonging to a larger community, beyond your individual personality, and having a sense of your place in creation.

You are congruent when all the different parts of you are working together in harmony. Then the music you play will be uniquely your own. Congruence means you are all of a piece, your body language, words and tonality all carry the same message, and your actions line up with your beliefs and values. You walk your talk – a shorthand way of saying your mind and body agree. Congruence is not an all or nothing state – there are degrees of congruence. Also, you may be congruent in some situations and incongruent in others.

The outside world mirrors your congruence. Internal conflicts provoke external ones. People who find it difficult to live with themselves are also difficult for others to live with and the quality of rapport we achieve with ourselves often mirrors the quality of rapport we achieve with others.

We all have different experiences, none of us sees the world in the same way and whatever is 'really' out there, each of us acts on what we perceive – that is reality for us. We make a model of the world from our life experiences, beliefs, values, interests and preoccupations and then we live it. This model of the world is not just an intellectual construct. it is a whole way of being in the world. It is a way of breathing, a way of walking, of talking, of how we relate to others and ourselves, and how we respond to stress. We embody it. Our model of the world, especially the beliefs and values, is one of the greatest influences on our health from moment to moment.

PACING

Rapport is achieved by pacing. Pacing others is acknowledging them and their concerns, being able to meet them in their model of the world, rather than demand they see things your way. Pacing is a good metaphor. Imagine walking alongside and talking to someone. To have a good conversation you both need to walk at the same speed – one that is comfortable for both of you. When you have something to say that you want them to hear, you walk at their pace.

Pacing is a very broad concept. It is respecting the customs of a foreign country. It is wearing appropriate clothes for meeting others. It is acknowledging the beliefs and values of others without trying to convince them they are wrong. Pacing is not the same as agreeing. You do not need to take on the beliefs of others to pace them, only acknowledge their importance and validity. You may still think they are mistaken. You will be clear about your own beliefs and values. Those people who are the most confident and congruent about their own beliefs and values are strong enough to allow others the space to hold different ones without having to argue or proselytize.

Once you have paced, you have established a bridge, a connection. Then you can lead – move yourself or others to a different more desirable state.

What does it mean to pace *yourself?* It means acknowledging what is there, without necessarily trying to change it. If you have a headache, it means acknowledging that and being aware of it. Pacing your body is being aware of its messages. Pacing your feelings means acknowledging them, not overriding them or acting on what you think you 'should' be feeling. Only after pacing will you seek to change them if you want to – to lead into another state.

When we are not feeling well, we may try to lead straightaway – to try and get rid of the feeling before even really knowing what it is. In doing this, we lose valuable knowledge – valuable because it may contain the key to avoiding that feeling next time. This is like trying to brusquely brush aside another person's feelings. We often treat ourselves in ways we would never treat others.

Pacing and leading is the key to influencing yourself and others. It does not usually work to lead someone before you have paced them. You may have had the experience of feeling ill or unhappy and another person, with the best of intentions, tells you, 'Buck up, pull yourself together, things aren't that bad!' This does not usually have the desired effect. It is as if they are ignoring your experience and so you have to insist on it even more. In an argument, a person who feels you have not understood their point of view will repeat it more emphatically. Our bodies act in the same way. If we ignore the signals of discomfort for long enough, they become stronger and more insistent – and this can lead to illness.

OUTCOMES

The second principle of NLP is knowing what you want. Unless you know where you are going you will wander aimlessly and not even know if you have arrived. NLP presupposes we act purposefully, although sometimes we are not clear what that purpose is. The clearer you are about what you want, the easier it is to achieve. The things you want are known in NLP as 'outcomes'.

Healing is a movement towards a state you want in the future and away from your unsatisfactory state in the present. It can be difficult to think about positive health and moving towards health goals, because the prevailing medical model encourages us to take health for granted when we have it and cure illness when we do not. Medicine studies illness, not health and how to achieve it. Preventative medicine, by its very name, deals with what not to do so that you will not get ill.

NLP looks at positive health in two ways. One is by exploring health as a positive state to be cultivated – modelling health. The second is to help build future outcomes – those things that are important to us and that we strive to achieve. A sense of purpose comes from attractive, even compelling future goals.

SENSORY ACUITY

The third pillar of NLP is sensory acuity – using your senses, being alert to the signals you are getting. Staying healthy means paying attention to what your body is giving you. It will tell you when you do something that is not good for it. Joseph smoked cigarettes for years, starting when he went to college. The first cigarette tasted appalling. It burnt his throat, made him cough and feel ill. However, he persevered and after a few weeks was able to smoke easily. It even felt pleasant. The first signals are always the most important. We can get used to almost anything given time. Your body will give you unmistakable signals that certain actions are hurting you. Sometimes they are immediate, sometimes they are more drawn out – continually overworking so you come home worn out, constantly drinking too much and waking up with a hangover, constantly overeating and feeling uncomfortable. It is persistently doing these things that does the damage. Eventually it comes to a head and you fall ill. This is the final signal, so strong that you cannot ignore it.

Sensory acuity is the key to pleasure. Puritanism still whispers in our ear that there must be something wrong in feeling good and all life's pleasures come with price tags. In fact following what feels good gives us immediate enjoyment and improves health. A good principle to follow is: whatever feels good is good for you when you are in a state of balance.

Pleasure comes from using the senses to the full – savouring a meal, seeking out beautiful surroundings, listening to music. The less acute your senses, the more you will resort to quantity rather than quality. The more acute your senses, the more possibility for pleasure.

USING YOUR SENSES – INSIDE AND OUTSIDE

To pace others and build rapport, you need to be aware of how they respond. Sensory acuity on the outside is paying attention to other people's responses, so you can respond in a way that will bring both of you closer to your goals. In many cultures children are trained *not* to notice this kind of information – it is too embarrassing for adults! However, if you are deaf and blind to your effect on others, how will you get the goals you want?

Try this experiment:

Look around you. See the people and objects that surround you. Look at the shapes and colours. Listen to the sounds, the voices, the music. Now pay attention to what you feel. How comfortable is your body? What sort of emotional state are you in?
Check your posture and balance.
Notice what you are tasting.
What do you smell?
Now try and recreate that memory. Close your eyes if this helps. Think back to that scene. See as much of it as you can remember. Then delete the picture. Blank it out, see darkness.
Next, wipe the sounds and voices that were in the scene from your memory or turn them down until they are inaudible. Then turn them off.
Next, erase any memory of the bodily feelings you had.
Lose any emotions you remember. Lastly lose the tastes and smells.
Is there anything left? A flickering image? A whisper of sound? Delete that as well. Come into the present moment and open your eyes.
Now, where is that experience?

Our experiences come through our senses. How vividly you remember that scene depends on the quality of attention you gave it at the time. You recreated it through those same senses. Your senses are your experience on the inside as well as the outside. Thinking is using your senses on the inside.

How you use your senses on the outside affects your thinking and experience on the inside.

You can change your experience by changing how you use your senses on the inside.

This has tremendous implications for health. It explains how some people can deal with stress while others become ill. Stress is not so much what happens to you but what you make of it and how you respond to it. Representing it differently to yourself will change your reaction. When you change your reaction, the stress may disappear. We will say much more on this in Chapter 8.

Our senses present us with information. We 're-present' our experience to ourselves using our senses and so in NLP the senses are called 'representational systems'.

There are five representational systems:

Sense	Representational System
Sight	Visual (abbreviated to V)
Hearing	Auditory (abbreviated to A)
Feeling	Kinesthetic (abbreviated to K)
Tasting	Gustatory (abbreviated to G)
Smell	Olfactory (abbreviated to O)

The visual system includes all our mental pictures, both remembered and constructed. The auditory system includes our memories of sounds, music and voices. It also includes our internal dialogue (or more often monologue) – talking to ourselves. The kinesthetic system is made up of our bodily feelings (proprioceptive), our sense of balance (vestibular), direct feelings of touch (tactile) and our emotions, although these latter are a little different. Emotions are how we feel about some issue and are made up of clusters of different proprioceptive feelings in our bodies.

We develop our senses on the outside – artists develop the ability to see, musicians the ability to hear, athletes a refined kinesthetic sense of their bodies – and on the inside, in the same way, we have one or two preferred representational systems with which we think. With a preference for the visual system you might be interested in design, fashion, the visual arts, television, mathematics and physics. With an auditory preference you may be interested in language, writing, drama, music and lecturing. A kinesthetic preference might be manifested in sport, carpentry and athletics. These are very general categories. It is futile to typecast people; we all use all the representational systems. However, we tend to favour one or two.

The more you use your senses on the outside and the more acute they are, the more you may favour them as representational systems. This gives us certain strengths and weaknesses in the ways we think. For some, thinking means mostly making vivid mental pictures. For others, it means conversations with themselves. For others, it is following their feelings. No way is right or wrong, it depends what you want to do. We also combine systems and think in 'synesthesias' – mixtures of systems where pictures, sounds and feelings are mixed together seamlessly.

Representational system preferences have consequences for your health. What are you missing? For example, a person who is weak in their visual representational system may find it difficult to visualize a good future. When illness strikes, they hope that they will recover. Hope comes from being able to visualize a better future. Without this, it is too easy to become depressed and lethargic.

A person who is weak in the auditory system may not be aware of their internal dialogue. Most of us talk to ourselves constantly. What sort of advice are we giving? What sort of voice tone are we using? What would be the effect of someone whispering in your ear in a unpleasant tone of voice that it is hard to be healthy? Not very helpful. Yet we may be doing this to ourselves.

A person who is less developed in the kinesthetic system may not be so aware of their body. They may push it past its limits or ignore symptoms until they are so unpleasant as to demand attention. This is like ignoring someone talking to you until they have to shout or not looking at them until they have grabbed you by the lapels.

Paying attention to what you see, hear and feel is just as important on the inside as on the outside.

FLEXIBILITY

The final pillar of NLP is flexibility of behaviour. When the feedback you get from your senses tells you that you are not getting what you want, you change your behaviour. It sounds obvious, but often people will not change, just keep on doing more of the same thing. This achieves variable outcomes and not necessarily the ones they want.

NLP recommends fixing your outcome and using all the varied means in your power to move towards it. This works for positive health and indeed for any outcome you want. Have as many choices as possible about how you achieve your outcome, and use your senses as feedback to let you know what brings you closer to it and what moves you away from it. If what you are doing is not working, do something else.

Flexibility comes from being clear about what you want and finding ways to achieve it. For example, if you are driving to work and the route is continually congested, you will probably find

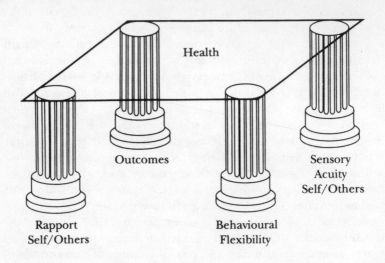

The four pillars of NLP

another route – that is, if you want to arrive on time. You would hardly stubbornly sit in the jam thinking to yourself, 'This is the way I've always come, so I'm going to stick to it.' Yet we sometimes do the equivalent of this with our health, because in health issues, cause and effect are neither so obvious nor so immediate. Also, habit and familiarity can seem so comfortable that we do not make the change our body demands.

So, for example, if you suffer from neck or back pain, you will want to explore different ways of sitting and standing or perhaps change your sleeping habits. If you suffer from indigestion, you may need to change your eating habits – changing the meals, times and speed of eating. With dermatitis you may need to experiment with different clothes fabrics and washing powders. Food allergies are difficult to pinpoint – you need systematically to give up various foods and then be sensitive to the effect that has. (Unfortunately, the guilty food is very often one of our favourites.)

A final example: a friend of Joseph's was a keen tennis player and enjoyed the sport very much. Playing provided good exercise too. He hurt his right elbow and for some weeks believed he could not play tennis (he was right-handed). The diagnosis was not good: the arm would take months to heal. It seemed he faced months of enforced inactivity. So he started to learn to play tennis left-handed. He said he found it fascinating to learn again from the beginning, and appreciated the skill and technique more. Because he had played a lot in the past right-handed, he learned very quickly and played left-handed for some months until his right arm was fully healed.

It may be hard to connect feedback with cause because of a long time delay. Physiological processes change slowly. Today's headache may be connected to yesterday's rich meal, but the connection is not obvious. So sometimes we persist in behaviour that does not enhance our health because the feedback occurs a long time afterwards. Also we may look in the wrong place. Our bodies and minds are inseparable, but we are used to thinking of them as separate. So food can cause mood swings, disturbed relationships can contribute to illness and it is hard to know exactly where to look. The mind moves fast. The body reacts more slowly but the reactions are deep.

We may be aware of an unhealthy habit yet find it hard to change. Behaviour, habits, beliefs and values all fit together in a complex system, each influencing the others. You cannot easily unbolt one bit without putting something else in its place. This is why so many health goals go astray. We may try to stop doing something without replacing it with something better and keeping the benefits we get from the old habit. The 'part' of us that is responsible for the old habit has not been consulted. It never agreed to stop.

Giving up smoking is a good example. In order to do it a person may need to do the following:

feel in their body that it is doing harm
believe it is doing them harm
adjust their breathing habits
deal with all the positive by-products of smoking that they value,
    for example being at ease in social situations, by finding
    another way of achieving them
break the automatic associations that trigger having a cigarette in
    particular circumstances, for example after a meal
form a new picture of themselves that is more in keeping with the
    person they really aspire to be who does not smoke
break any link between smoking and identity, such as thinking of
    themselves as a smoker

engage the support of their friends and family

finally be aware of the money they are saving and use it on something positive that they value

EMOTIONAL STATE

Your emotional state in the present moment is a snapshot of your health.

In NLP, a state is your way of being at any moment, the sum of your thoughts, feelings, emotions, mental and physical energy. It includes both mind and body, both your mental and physiological way of being. Some states are intense and obvious – for example, anger, love, boredom, jealousy and joy. We notice the highs and lows, the peaks and valleys of our emotional life. We may not even have a name for the state we are in, but it will have its characteristic way of thinking, feeling and emotional tone. States are the internal environment and we can become habituated to them just as we can to an external environment – after a while we just do not notice it. So there is a danger that we may get used to a chronic low state that chips away at our health and well-being.

There is abundant evidence that a chronic state of hostility and impatience is associated with increased risk of heart attacks and coronary artery blockages.[4] Chronic, serious depression has been associated with an increased risk of cancer[5] and in one study, depression proved to be a better predictor of heart problems than severity of artery damage, high cholesterol levels or cigarette smoking.[6]

Many studies have shown that depression lowers immune response. Prolonged negative states are bad for your health. And the converse is true: positive states are good for health. They feel good and we seek them out, so it is no surprise that medicine has made it scientifically respectable to feel good. For example, in one study people who had been watching a video of the

4   *There is a thorough review of the link between hostility and cardiovascular disease in* Chesney, M., and Rosenman R. (eds), *Anger and Hostility in Cardiovascular and Behavioural Disorders*, Hemisphere Publishing Corporation, 1985.

5   Persky, V., Kempthorne-Rawson, J., and Shekelle, R., 'Personality and risk of cancer: 20 year follow-up of the Western Electric Study, *Psychosomatic Medicine* 49 (1987), 435–49

6   Carney, R. *et al.*, *Psychosomatic Medicine* (1989)

comedian Richard Pryor boosted their immune system as measured by the level of antibodies in their saliva.[7] These antibodies help defend against infections like the common cold. The immune boost lasted for an hour. Those subjects who said they often used humour as a way of coping with stress had consistently higher baseline levels of these protective antibodies. Writer Norman Cousins attributed his cure from the crippling disease Alkylosing Spondylitis in large part to watching comedy videos.[8] Laughter heals.

It is not surprising that a strong negative state such as depression should depress the immune system. What is interesting is that even mimicking emotions can have an effect on the body. Paul Ekman, a psychologist at the University of California in San Francisco, has done several studies of facial expressions, specializing in those that people use when they lie.[9] In one study he asked actors to mimic facial expressions of disgust, anger and fear or to relive one of those experiences in their minds. Ekman measured heartbeat and skin temperature and was able to identify which particular negative emotion the actor was miming by these measurements. Pretending to be angry or reliving an experience mentally had direct physiological effects on the body through the autonomic nervous system.

A chronic negative state is rather like walking 'close to the edge' – it is much easier to lose balance. A gust of wind that would be no trouble if we were well balanced could blow us off.

Being ill is an unmistakable change of state, although many of the unpleasant symptoms of illness – coughs, inflammation, high temperature, sickness, aching joints – are actually caused by the body trying to heal itself. These symptoms are often necessary to rebalance again.

MOOD FOOD

Food is psycho-active. It affects our state as well as nourishing us. Any law that tried to ban all psycho-active substances would make food illegal! Nerve cells throughout the body communicate with

7 Dillon, K., Minchoff, B., and Baker, K., 'Positive emotional states and enhancement of the immune system', *International Journal of Psychiatry in Medicine* 15 (1985–6), 13–17
8 Cousins, Norman, *Anatomy of an Illness as Perceived by the Patient*, Norton, 1979
9 Ekman, Paul *et al.*, *Emotion in the Human Face*, Pergamon, 1972

each other using substances called 'neurotransmitters'. These are the way our body passes messages through nerves that reach our awareness as thoughts and feelings. They are where mind and body merge. Neurotransmitters are made from precursors contained in foods we eat.

There are many different kinds of neurotransmitters. For example, serotonin is one important inhibitory neurotransmitter that reduces nerve activity and initiates sleep. Tryptophan is an amino acid that the brain uses to make serotonin, and milk and bananas contain relatively large amounts of tryptophan, so hot milk at bedtime really does help you to fall asleep. A meal rich in carbohydrates such as bread and potatoes raises serotonin levels, a meal rich in protein depresses serotonin levels by stopping the brain from using tryptophan. The brain balances and regulates the protein and carbohydrate we consume partly through the levels of serotonin. A carbohydrate snack can actually make us feel more relaxed and peaceful – the 'siesta feeling'. The mechanism is quite complex because other amino acids compete with tryptophan for transport to the brain. Carbohydrate consumption can also, through its effect on serotonin levels, cause feelings of fatigue, and make it easier to tolerate mild pain and discomfort.

What you eat for lunch affects more than your physical fitness. Food can very quickly affect your attention span and memory. Neurotransmitters in the brain can be enhanced by diet. When you feel irritable or tense, then carbohydrate snacks can help. They are a form of self-medication. Unfortunately, there is a side-effect of habitual carbohydrate snacks on the waistline.

Eating changes our state and changing state always corresponds with a change in our internal biochemistry, especially the balance of different neurotransmitters. These natural substances are powerful, but the body's pharmacy only dispenses them in small quantities. Your body is the best prescriber. It adjusts the dosage to exactly your need.

There are plenty of substances we use to change state directly, from chocolate, coffee, tea and alcohol all the way through to cocaine and heroin. Drugs and diets are a vast and complicated subject, and not one we will address in this book. From the NLP point of view, our state varies throughout the day. There are ways in which we seek to change it, sometimes unconsciously through food, sometimes consciously through drugs. Indeed, some drug-induced states seem so valuable that some people will even risk painful, sometimes fatal side-effects.

NLP looks at the ways we can change state through our thoughts.

If state is so closely related to health, then the ability to change state by choice is invaluable if you want to stay healthy. NLP has studied this in depth. We will look at it in the next chapter.

FOOD FOR THOUGHT

Health is the state about which medicine has nothing to say.

W. H. Auden

Every man takes the limits of his own field of vision for the limits of the world.

Arthur Schopenhauer

Even if you are on the right track, you will get run over if you just sit there.

Will Rogers

By nature, men are nearly alike. By practice they get to be wide apart.

Confucius

A PICTURE OF HEALTH

To pace your own emotional state, you need to discover the state where you spend most of your time – what we call your 'baseline state'. This sets your characteristic way of being, breathing, posture and expression. Joseph was brought literally face to face with his in Denver, Colorado, some years ago. There were street artists in the central plaza who did caricatures for a few dollars. Joseph looked at the picture of himself the artist had sketched. He saw a man with rounded shoulders and a stooped posture. Who was that stranger? He felt the same way as when he heard his voice on tape for the first time. The impression made an impression. Joseph took up lessons in Alexander technique bodywork to improve his habitual posture.

If you know your baseline state, are you happy with it? How do you like its architecture, furnishings and amenities? Do you notice them any more? Time for stocktaking. Any place you spend a lot of time needs to be as comfortable and pleasant as possible, particularly as it affects your health.

YOUR BASELINE STATE

Take a few minutes to explore your baseline state now, using your sensory acuity on the inside.

Sit down comfortably and take stock of your state from different points of view:

What is your habitual posture?
What does it feel like?

What would a caricature bring out?
Is the state light or heavy?
Do you have a predominant expression?
How does it manifest in the way you walk?
In the way you sit?
In the way you talk?

If you are brave enough, ask other people for their perceptions too.

What do you like about it?
Are there parts of it that you would like to change?

Where do you habitually breathe? (You can tell because other ways will be an effort and will feel different.)
Is it high in the chest or lower in the abdomen?

When your baseline state has been there for a long time it can seem the only way to be, instead of just one of the many ways you could be.

Your Thoughts and Emotions

What is your predominant emotion?
What sort of thoughts are you predominately aware of?
Do you visualize a lot?
Do you talk to yourself a great deal?
Do outside events touch you deeply or can you keep your emotional distance?

Your Relationships with Others

Do you find yourself mostly in the company of people you enjoy?
What emotions do other people elicit in you?

The Origins of your Baseline State

Do you have an idea where it comes from?
Can you trace it back to a particular incident or decision you made in the past?

Does this decision still hold?
Have you had it a long time or have you changed it recently?
Have you modelled it from somebody, perhaps a parent or
significant person in your life? (When we model beliefs, values
and ways of acting from others we often get the state that goes
with it without noticing.)

Even thinking about these questions without getting a definite
answer will make you more aware of your state.

DESIGN YOUR OWN BASELINE STATE

Once you know something of your baseline state, you can
customize it.

What do you like about your present baseline state?

Make sure you keep these things if you plan to change.

What do you dislike about your present baseline state
and seek to change?

What qualities do you want to add?

Do you have any role models for these qualities?

What physiology would you like to have?

You may want to find out about different kinds of bodywork, for example Alexander technique or Feldenkreis
work, to change habitual postures and ways of using your
body.

Designing a baseline state that you like may take some
time. It is not something you can do in a few minutes. So
take time over the weeks ahead. Your baseline state is like
your psychological house. You spend a lot of time there,
so make it as comfortable and healthy as possible.

Have something to remind you of the changes you are
making. Pick something you see or hear every day.
Whenever you see or hear the reminder, check your state.
Joseph put up his caricature on the living-room wall.
A friend of ours turned a picture on his wall upside-down.
Being a tidy man, he keeps noticing it and wants to
correct it. This reminds him to check his state. He
promised himself he will correct the picture when he has
a new baseline state he is happy with.

ANCHORS

People, places, particular sights and sounds can change our state automatically. These are known as 'anchors'. In NLP, an anchor is any sight, sound or touch that triggers a state. Anchors are built by repetition and association. For example, when a friend of Ian's went to see his daughter's teacher at her primary school, he was struck by how the sights, sounds and smells of school took him back for a moment to how he felt when he was at primary school, many years ago.

The power of anchors is based on our ability to learn by making links and forming associations. They make it easy to react without thinking. Ringing a bell means the end of a school lesson, so everyone switches off even though the teacher may keep talking. A red traffic light means stop. We do not want to have to think every time we approach a traffic light and search our memory for what to do.

Anchors are ubiquitous – the national anthem, a fire alarm, a baby's smile. Some anchors are neutral – we just react, for example the red traffic light. Some have the power to put us in a negative state – spiders do this to many people. Others are positive, associated with good states – for example the voice of someone we love. None of these things carry the feeling in themselves – a spider is just a spider, a voice is a voice. We add the significance.

We create our own anchors or learn them from society. They are mostly built at random. Sometimes, as in phobias, one intense experience can create an anchor immediately. A young child may be intensely frightened by a snake, being too young to evaluate the danger realistically. From then on, seeing any snake evokes that frightened state. An anchor has the power to transport you back, just as Ian's friend was to his primary school.

Once established, anchors act automatically. That is their advantage and danger: an advantage if we use them for positive states and a danger if they put us unaware into negative states. We will have many anchors for our habitual baseline state.

We give anchors the power to elicit states. Beware of those that put you in negative states and cultivate those that put you in positive ones. What sort of an anchor is a visit to the doctor? Anchors can be visual, such as the spider, a bunch of flowers, a green traffic light or a full moon. They can be auditory, like the sound of a dentist's drill (sets your teeth on edge!), a special song or a fire alarm. They can be kinesthetic, like a handshake or a hot bath. They can be olfactory, like the smell of coffee or the smell of a hospital corridor. Gustatory anchors could be Swiss chocolate or a pint of beer. They can be in the external environment, but they can also be internal. For example, imagining the smell of coffee, or the sound of chalk scraping across a blackboard, or visualizing a spider will still evoke the anchored state, although not usually as intensely as the real thing. The brain reacts to an anchor whether it comes from the outside or the inside. Our body–mind reacts to what it perceives as real.

Anchors operate at every logical level. Our name is an anchor for our identity and religious icons anchor beliefs. Companies pay thousands of pounds for logos and advertising to create anchors that associate their product with a desirable state – sexual attractiveness, freedom, sophistication. They pay famous entertainers huge sums of money to endorse their product. The money is for the good feelings already anchored to those entertainers that hopefully will be transferred to the product – success by association. Sponsorship works the same way.

Words can be anchors too. When we write about spiders and chocolate, those are ink marks on paper. You create the pictures, sounds and feelings in your mind to understand the words.

IMMUNE SYSTEM ANCHORS

Anchors change our state and our state affects our health. Medical research is beginning to understand exactly how. There is evidence that anchors can directly affect our immune system. The initial discovery gave rise to a whole new field of medicine – Psychoneuroimmunology (PNI) – the exploration of how our beliefs, behaviour and environment affect our immune system. In NLP terms, PNI is the relationship between logical levels and the immune system. Our immune system is the part that protects us by destroying antigens, bacteria, viruses and cancer cells. Measuring the strength of the immune system is one of the most direct ways that medicine can measure how healthy we are.

In the mid 1970s, psychologist Robert Ader at the University of Rochester was investigating the influence of psychosocial factors – behaviour, beliefs and relationships – on health.[1] Ader was doing some simple stimulus–response experiments with rats, trying to condition them to associate a feeling of nausea with saccharin-flavoured water. The rats drank the water and then were injected with a powerful drug that causes nausea. One trial was enough for the rats to get the point. Saccharin meant sickness.

The flavoured water alone without the injection of the drug was then sufficient to make the rats nauseous. Saccharin water had been made into a gustatory anchor for nausea. The experiment was a straightforward success. However, there was an unusual side-effect: many of the rats died. Ader could not understand it – they were healthy and well cared for throughout the experiment.

The answer was in the substance that produced the nausea – Cyclophosphamide. This powerful drug not only causes vomiting, it also suppresses the immune system. The saccharin water had become an anchor not only for nausea but also for a weakened immune system. The rats were conditioned to suppress their immune system whenever they drank the saccharin-flavoured water. This left them more open to infection and many more died than expected.

Ader and his colleague Nicholas Cohen successfully tested this hypothesis in a series of experiments. The results were consistent. The conditioned rats succumbed more easily to infectious diseases than the controls. They also became more resistant to autoimmune diseases such as arthritis. This made sense – a weaker immune system would not attack its own body so strongly. Ader coined the term 'Psychoneuroimmunology' for the study of the interaction between the immune system, the nervous system and states of mind.[2]

We are not yet sure exactly how these results apply to human behaviour, but the implications are fascinating. They suggest how negative states are translated into illness. We know that depression, loneliness, anxiety and hostility can damage your health. The anchors for the states may also anchor a weaker immune system

---

1 Ader, R., 'Behavioural conditioning and the immune system' in Temoshok, L., Van Dyke, C., and Zegans, L. (eds), *Emotions in Health and Illness*, Gruner and Stratton, 1983
2 Ader, R. (ed.), *Psychoneuroimmunology*, Academic Press, 1981

response. For Ader's rats an anchor was the difference between life and death.

Negative anchors may weaken your immune system and leave you more open to illness.

The good news is that it can work the other way too – positive anchors can strengthen the immune system. How would it change your life if you could hear a piece of music, look at a photograph and not only feel good, but know that you were strengthening your immune system and so building positive health for yourself?

CHANGING STATE

States affect your health and anchors affect states.

Three important questions follow:

- What triggers my negative states?
- When I am in a negative state, how can I change it?
- How can I create more positive, healthy states for myself?

To have more choice about your emotional state, identify your negative anchors. What sights, sounds, tastes, smells and touches put you in an unresourceful state? (Irritation, hostility, depression, feeling helpless, harassed or fearful are examples of unresourceful states. Sad states are not necessarily unresourceful.) Is your negative anchor a particular tone of voice? A particular facial expression? The sound of rain first thing in the morning? A full in-tray?

When you notice the anchor you have taken a significant step towards breaking its hold. Start by pacing yourself. Pay attention to how you feel. Ask yourself, 'Do I *need* to feel this way?' 'Do I *want* to feel this way?'

When you find yourself in an unresourceful state there are two options. First you can simply stay with it in an interested way. Pace yourself. Notice which parts of your body are involved in it and which are not. Being with the state in this way can cause it to change and evolve. You may feel tired and feel like relaxing for a few minutes. You may feel renewed energy. Your state will change once you give it your attention.

Secondly, you can change state in a more direct way. Once you are out of the unresourceful state you can address any problem that put you in that state. Do not attempt to resolve a problem *in* the unresourceful state. Change state first, otherwise the state will cast a pall over your thinking.

There are two ways to change state that do not involve food or drugs:

• change your physiology
• change your thinking

The first thing to do when you find yourself in an unresourceful state is to immediately do something different. One of the best ways is to change your breathing pattern. All states have a characteristic breathing pattern. For example, when you are anxious or panicky you hyperventilate (i.e. you breathe quickly with a short exhale). This produces biochemical changes that increase your feeling of anxiety. The anxious feeling increases the breathing rate and a fast breathing rate compounds the anxiety. To feel calmer, slow your breathing, take twice as long to exhale as to inhale. Laughter is the best for changing your state – it plays havoc with your breathing pattern (and thinking), in the nicest possible way. Physical movement is another way to change state. Moving around, going for a walk and exercising all work well.

States organize your physiology in a characteristic way. Changing physiology changes state. This may be why *pretending* to be happy can actually have real physical effects. Changing thinking will not work unless it brings a shift in physiology – whether deliberate or involuntary is irrelevant.

Building a Resourceful State

Sometimes you will want to build a resourceful state directly. You might like to experiment with resourceful states as you would with a wardrobe of clothes, 'trying them on for size'. There are three ways to do this:

• *Pick a role model.*
  The role model can be a real person or a fictional character. Pick one or several characters who have qualities that you would like. What would it be like to take on those qualities?

- *Physiology.*
Acting as if you feel resourceful will trigger resourceful feelings.
Stooping, looking down, slumping and sighing are all likely to
trigger depressing thoughts. The depressing thoughts cause a
further slump and hence more depressing thoughts. That is a
vicious circle. You can start a *virtuous* circle by standing up, looking up, breathing deeply and smiling. This is likely to trigger
good feelings. You are not being phoney – you know that you do
not feel happy (yet). You are simply changing your state.

- *Good past experiences.*
Think back to a really pleasant experience. Go back in your
mind to that scene. See it again through your own eyes, hear
any sounds that are there. The good feelings will return as
well. Our brain responds to the memory of an event in the
same way it responded to the actual event. This is how anchors
work. A piece of music, a photograph, a smell can take you
right back into the experience again. This is the basis for lucky
charms. They are anchors for good past experiences and so
the person feels lucky in the present. They work not by magic,
but by association. Whatever the resourceful feeling, if you
have had a glimpse or a whisper of it in the past, you can bring
it into the present.

Create an anchor for this good experience, so that you can
bring it into the present any time you choose. It is best to use
something that is naturally associated with the memory – a
picture, a piece of music, some kind of memento. If there is
nothing like this available, create an association. Decide on the
anchor you want. Every time you see it, go back in your mind
and re-experience the memory, be back inside it and feel the
emotions again.

Anchors need practice, but when you have done this for a few
days, the association will happen naturally and automatically,
and you will no longer have to think consciously of the experience. The good feelings will come of themselves whenever you
see, hear, feel or taste the anchor.

ASSOCIATION AND DISSOCIATION

NLP is the study of the structure of subjective experience. There are two fundamentally different ways in which states can be structured and the best way to appreciate them is through experience.

Think of a sad experience – an upset, rather than a major trauma. As you do, notice whether you are seeing yourself in the experience, as on a television or film screen, or whether you are actually inside the experience, looking out of your own eyes, having the same view as when it happened.
You may be flipping quickly between the two.
Now break state. Move your body, shake off the sad experience and think of something else for a moment.

Now think of a really good experience, one you really enjoyed. As you go back to that, notice again whether you are seeing yourself in the picture or whether you are actually inside the experience.
Now break state again and come back to the present.

When you are looking at yourself in the experience from another vantage point, you are *dissociated* from it. When you are back in the experience, looking through your own eyes, seeing, hearing and feeling as if you are there, then you are *associated* into it.

The most important difference is that when you are associated, you get the feelings of the experience. When you are dissociated you automatically reduce those feelings.

Choosing whether to associate or dissociate in a memory gives a great deal of emotional freedom. When you remember pleasant experiences, associate. Then you will get the good feelings that come with them. When you think back to unpleasant experiences, dissociate. Then you will be able to keep your emotional distance and learn from them.

It is hard to learn from our mistakes if we associate back into the experiences. We get the intense unpleasant feelings and jump back to the present. (This is why phobias are so resilient – the feelings are so intense and traumatic that it is almost impossible to go back and re-evaluate the initial experience. NLP can heal phobias quickly by using dissociation to neutralize the experience and learn from it. The alternative is usually months of desensitizing therapy, essentially breaking the anchor and replacing it with a new one.) When you associate back into a negative state you are putting your body through this same unpleasant sensation again and again. This is unnecessary. There is a wise saying: 'Those who do not learn from the past are doomed to repeat it.' Once you have learned from an unpleasant experience, you will spontaneously store it as a dissociated picture.

Association and dissociation are ways of being. When you are intensely in the moment, enjoying sensual pleasures, you are associated, at least we hope so, else you are missing a lot. When you are reflective, you are dissociated. Dissociation protects us from shock and trauma, we are 'not really there'.

Association is not better than dissociation, it depends what you want to do. If you want to analyse and learn from experience, then dissociate. If you want to 'be here, now' in the present moment, then associate.

LEARNING FROM EXPERIENCE

Think of a past negative experience, perhaps connected with a health issue.

Go back to the experience for a moment or two and notice whether you are associated or dissociated. If you are associated, then dissociate. You can do this by stepping out of yourself and continuing to watch. You could also do it by pushing yourself and any other people in the picture away from you. You could do it another way by taking another perspective on the scene, perhaps looking down from the ceiling.

If you are already dissociated, then change your viewpoint. Look at the scene from a radically different angle.

Now, as you look at yourself in that situation and watch it play out before you, ask yourself, 'What can I learn from that experience?'

Notice how your feelings change once you have the learning.

REAL IMAGINARY FRUIT

Our thoughts directly affect our bodies through our representational systems. Imagine for a moment that you are holding one of your favourite fruits in your hand. Imagine yourself feeling its weight and texture. Is it hard or soft when you squeeze? What colour do you imagine it to be? Say the name of the fruit to yourself. Now close your eyes and imagine yourself smelling it. How does the smell make you feel? Now you are going to taste it. Mentally peel it if necessary and bring it slowly towards your mouth. Take a bite out of it so you can feel the juice under your tongue.

If you did not salivate at all, you must be asleep. Smells and tastes are particularly evocative.

Your brain does not recognize a difference between body and mind. The more you dwell on something happening, the more the body–mind responds as if it were actually happening. Think of the health implications of this simple experiment with imaginary fruit:

What we think directly affects our bodies.
The more vividly we think, the more the body responds.

So, creating strong, vivid representations of health will be useful. And the more clearly and easily you can use all the representational systems, the more control you will have over their effect on your body. Using the representational systems consciously like this may seem strange at first, but practice makes it easier.

People differ in their ability to use different representational systems. Some do not see clear mental pictures and a small percentage claim they make no pictures at all. This is true for them – that is their experience. What it means is that they are not conscious of their mental pictures. We all visualize, otherwise we would not recognize our own face, car or front door.

If you have difficulty visualizing, try this experiment. Start by perceiving one piece of coloured glass in your mind. Write down or describe on tape what you see, even if it is only a glimpse. If this is difficult, pretend you can see it in your mind's eye. What colour is it? How big? What shape?

Now imagine the sound of a guitar. How loud is it in your mind? Can you turn up the volume? Is the sound high or low? Hear the rhythm of the music. Is it being played quickly or slowly? What would this guitar look like? Describe it to yourself.

Now imagine lying down comfortably. What are the feelings in your body? Imagine what your surroundings look like and the sounds you remember there, like the ticking of an alarm clock.

To help you think more vividly and clearly you can use the body–mind connection. When you want to visualize, defocus your eyes or turn your head and look upwards. To hear internal sounds more clearly, turn your head to one side and look across to your left. To engage in internal dialogue more clearly, look down to your left. To feel more intensely, look down to your right.

You have probably noticed people move their eyes as they think. These movements are not random, the eyes do not flop around in their sockets under the influence of gravity! There is meaning to the movements. They are known as 'eye accessing cues' and are another way our mind and body work together. NLP suggests that most people look up or defocus to visualize and look sideways to hear internal sounds. Most people look down to the right to access their feelings and down to the left to listen to their internal dialogue. For some, this pattern is reversed: they look down to the left for feelings and down right for self talk.

Eye accessing cues have many practical uses and are explained in detail in other books on NLP.[3] Experiment with them, they are useful to help you see, hear and feel more easily on the inside.

SUBMODALITIES

Any distinctions we make through our senses in the outside world, we can also make in our inner world. The distinctions we make in our mental pictures, sounds and feelings are called 'submodalities'. They are the qualities of our inner world, the smallest building blocks of our experience.

Colour and movement are examples of visual submodalities – two qualities

---

3   *See* O'Connor, J., and Seymour, J., *Introducing NLP*, Thorsons, 1990, *and* O'Connor, J., and McDermott, I., *Principles of NLP*, Thorsons, 1996

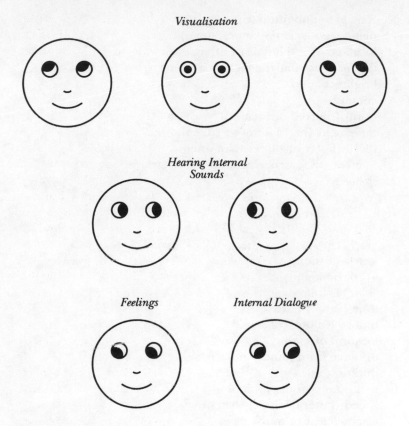

Eye accessing cues
N.B. This is as you look at the other person

of internal pictures. Volume and direction are examples of auditory submodalities, and temperature and pressure are kinesthetic submodalities.

Here are some of the most common submodality distinctions:

VISUAL SUBMODALITIES

associated (seen through own eyes) or dissociated (looking on at self)
colour or black and white

framed or unbounded
depth (two- or three-dimensional)
location (e.g. to left or right, up or down)
distance (how far the picture is from you)
brightness
contrast
clarity (blurred or focused)
movement (like a film or a slide show)
speed (faster or slower than usual)
number (split screen or multiple images)
size

AUDITORY SUBMODALITIES

stereo or mono
words or sounds
volume (loud or soft)
tone (soft or harsh)
timbre (fullness of sound)
location of sound
distance from sound source
duration
continuous or discontinuous
speed (faster or slower than usual)
clarity (clear or muffled)

KINESTHETIC SUBMODALITIES

location
intensity
pressure (hard or soft)
extent (how big)
texture (rough or smooth)
weight (light or heavy)
temperature
duration
shape

Submodalities are how we code experiences. All our memories, hopes, beliefs and fears have a submodality structure. When we change the submodalities, we change the structure of our experience and with it the meaning. When the meaning changes, our internal response will also change.

Review the picture of a pleasant experience. Notice the colour, brightness and the position in space. Now review an unpleasant experience. Many people see a darker picture with less movement, in a slightly different place. What difference do you see?

We began this book with an example of the submodality difference between 'health' and 'being healthy'.

Submodalities give you control over your internal experience. They are one way of applying flexibility to thinking in the pursuit of health.

TIMELINES

We use a rich range of submodality expressions to talk about time. We speak of the 'dim and distant past', 'a great future lies ahead', 'looking back and laughing' and 'time standing still'. Whatever time really is, we seem to think about it spatially.

How do you organize time in your mind so you can tell memories from future hopes? How do you know something happened yesterday as opposed to five years ago? You give them different submodalities.

Think of a past experience. Point to the direction it seems to come from. Now, think of some future plans or hopes. Which direction do those seem to come from? Imagine a line that connects past to future. That is your timeline.

Many people have a timeline with the past on the left, the present moment in front and the future off to the right. This is called 'through time'. The other common arrangement is to have the past behind you, the future in front of you and the present moment inside your body. This is known as 'in time'.

Timelines are fascinating. They have many uses and implications.[4] Most important for positive health is to be able to see a future that draws you forward. How far ahead does your future extend and does it look inviting? Timeline work is important with

4 *See* James, T., *Timeline Therapy and the Basis of Personality*, Meta Publications, 1988, *also* O'Connor, J., and Seymour, J., *Introducing NLP*, Thorsons, 1990

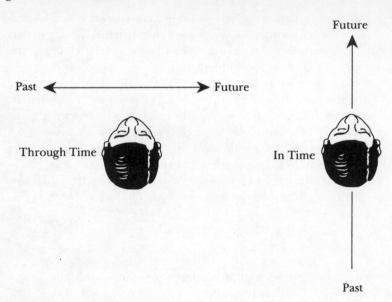

In time and through time timelines

seriously ill patients, because hope comes from being able to 'see' a future and clean up the past.

PAST, PRESENT AND FUTURE HEALTH

In the first chapter, you outlined what being healthy meant to you. Now you can make it real. Your definition may have used some abstract words like 'happiness', 'fitness' or 'wellness'. What do your words mean in experience?

Make a picture of yourself being healthy – really healthy. Make it a dissociated picture. What do you see? It does not matter exactly what you are doing in the picture, as long as you are satisfied that the picture means you are positively healthy. You may be 'glowing with health'.

Now, go through the list of visual submodalities *(see p.49)* and experiment by changing your picture to make it even more expressive of your vibrant health. For example, the first submodality in the list is colour. If your picture is in colour, then change it to black and white, if it is black and white, add colour.

Which is more appealing?
The next submodality is framed or unbounded.
If your picture is framed, take the frame away.
If it is unbounded, add a frame.
How do you feel about the change?
Go through all the submodalities and keep any changes that enhance the positive feeling the picture gives you.

Now hear any sounds that are in your picture.
Use the auditory submodality list to experiment *(see p.50)*. Can you enhance the good feelings through what you hear? Keep the changes you like.

Associate into the picture. You can do this either by stepping into your image or drawing the image into yourself in your imagination.
Check your feelings. Is this a really positive healthy state for you?
Is there anything you could do to improve it?
If there is, step out again and continue to experiment with the submodalities until you are satisfied.

When you are satisfied, you have found what being healthy means to you as a subjective experience – you have made the words real.
Make a list of your submodalities of positive health. You can use them in the future any time you wish to visualize healing.
The next stage is to put the dissociated picture in your timeline and leave it there.

Imagine your timeline stretching out before you. Take your picture and sounds of being healthy and put them into your future by placing them on the future part of your timeline.
How do you feel about what you see?
How do you relate to that future healthy you?
Does it seem realistic and attainable?
How far into the future did you put the picture?
Is there anything that might stop you attaining that future?

Experiment by putting the picture at different points in your future.
Place it one week from now.
One month from now.

One year from now.

Three years from now.

Five years from now.

Do you have different reactions?

What relationship do you want to establish with this healthy you in the future?

Do you feel drawn to that future?

What steps do you need to take in order to reach that future you?

What would you say to that future you?

What questions would you ask them?

Now go and become that future healthy you.

Associate into that future you.

Now, as that 'future you', look back on the 'present you'.

What do you feel?

What advice could you give that present you so they can reach where you are standing?

What reply would you give to the questions you have been asked?

What questions would you ask them?

Finally, step to one side and imagine you can see both the future really healthy you in the future and the present you.

What is the connection between them?

What can you learn from both of them?

Step back into the present you.

This exercise is very powerful. In it, being healthy becomes uniquely real to you.

With representational systems and submodalities you can fine-tune and shape being healthy to exactly how you want it. By placing it on your timeline in the future, you establish a relationship between you now and who you wish to be. You can see what needs to change and how to start.

FOOD FOR THOUGHT

The unhappy person is the target for any and every type of illness.

> B. Larson, *There's a Lot More to Health Than Not Being Sick*
> (Word Books, 1984)

A cheerful heart is good medicine, but a downcast spirit dries up the bones.

> Proverbs 17:22

If I told patients to raise their blood levels of immune globulins, or killer T-cells, no-one would know how. But if I can teach them to love themselves and others fully, the same changes happen automatically. The truth is: Love heals.

> Bernie Siegel, *Love, Medicine and Miracles* (Harper and Row, 1986)

Experimental and clinical psychologists have proved beyond a shadow of doubt that the human nervous system cannot tell the difference between an 'actual' experience and an experience imagined vividly and in detail.

> Maxwell Maltz, *Psycho-Cybernetics* (Prentice-Hall, 1960)

The art of medicine consists of amusing the patient while nature cures the disease.

> Voltaire

BELIEFS AND HEALTH

Beliefs are our guiding principles. We act as if they are true, whether they are or not. NLP takes a pragmatic view of beliefs – they are the principles we *act* on, not necessarily what we say we believe. Beliefs are generalizations, based on past experience, shaping future reactions. They are not facts, although we tend to notice supporting facts and explain away contradictions. Nor are they logical. They cannot be proved. They are the working hypotheses we bring to everyday life.

How healthy do you believe yourself to be? There are a number of fascinating studies by epidemiologists[1] where people have been asked to rate their overall health as either excellent, good, fair or poor. This self-rating was found to be an excellent prediction of how long they lived. The results held true even when gender, education, income and age were held constant. Everything else being equal, those people who *believed* they were in poor health were three times more likely to die in the subsequent seven years. What we believe about our health can be more influential than objective health measurements.

How is it possible for people with arthritis and high blood pressure to rate their health as good, while others who suffer only mild colds rate their health as poor? Because health is a subjective experience, your everyday reality, not something that can be measured and compared with others.

How healthy you believe yourself to be depends on the

1 Kaplan, G., and Camacho, T., 'Perceived health and mortality: a nine year follow-up of the human population laboratory cohort', *American Journal of Epidemiology* 11 (1983), 292–304
also Mossey, J., and Shapiro, E., 'Self-rated health: a predictor of mortality among the elderly', *American Journal of Public Health* 72 (1982), 800–8

evidence you have for health and the comparisons you make. It is important to be realistic. When health equals five years without any sort of illness plus the ability to run a marathon, then few people are likely to define themselves as healthy. However, if health is defined as balance and the ability to heal yourself, then it is possible to be a fundamentally healthy person who happens to be ill. Unrealistic comparisons influence our perceptions and our perceptions influence our health.

How you define health for yourself affects how healthy you believe you are.

How healthy you believe you are affects how long you live.

CAUSE AND EFFECT

Beliefs try to explain cause and effect. Cause and effect is a good principle when one follows the other quickly and without fail. When you cut your hand, it bleeds immediately. The further apart in time two events are, the less easily you can say that one 'caused' the other, for then many other events will have entered the chain.

It is very difficult to make any simple cause–effect statements about health. The human body is one of the most complex systems in the known universe and there tend to be multiple causes and associations. Some factors are necessary but not sufficient for illness. The influenza virus 'causes' 'flu – but only when many other factors are present, else everyone in the world would suffer constantly.

The human body works as a system, always trying to heal itself, even when it seems to be doing the opposite. For example, osteoporosis is a progressive reduction in bone density. The body takes calcium from the bones and they become ever more brittle. Why should the body take calcium from the bones? To stay alive. It needs a certain level for proper nerve functions. Your life is dependent on the body using calcium. When the body is unable to absorb adequate levels of calcium from the diet, it has to take it from the bones. Our diet does contain adequate calcium, provided the body is able to absorb it, but many foods make it hard for the body to utilize. Cow's milk contains a great deal of calcium but also a level of phosphorus that is high enough to interfere with calcium intake. Animal protein also interferes with calcium intake. The more animal protein you consume, the more calcium you excrete. A typical Western diet contains 300 per cent of the protein we need for an adequate diet. A diet that contains adequate calcium does not help if the body cannot absorb it. There may be a significant dietary component to osteoporosis.

Many symptoms are the body's attempt to heal itself. Inflammation helps to bring more blood and lymph to the site of damage. High temperature and fever allow the immune system to work more quickly. When we have an infection, our bodies produce chemicals that raise the level of our temperature control 'thermostat' in the hypothalamus of the brain. When the immune system has overcome the infection, these chemicals are no longer produced and the body sweats in an attempt to cool itself down.

BELIEFS AND MEANING

Beliefs give experiences meaning, they offer stability and understanding, and this explains why people will take a certain grim satisfaction if they can say 'I knew that would happen' when disaster strikes. Beliefs form a system, they fit together to form a structure that gives coherence to our experiences.

Sometimes changing one belief throws others into question. For example, if emotions can strengthen or depress the immune system that *means* I do have some control over when I am ill.

Serious illness often disrupts beliefs. A diagnosis of cancer, for example, is a shockingly direct belief change. Even trivial illnesses have meaning. How do you react when you are ill? Is it a shock? Are you annoyed? Is illness something to be got rid of as quickly as possible so you can go back to how you were before? Do you feel you must carry on as normal? Is illness a sign of weakness? Many people are unsympathetic to others who are ill; they believe that if they themselves can soldier on, so should everyone else.

Beliefs influence recovery from illness. Between 20 and 30 per cent of people who have a heart attack never make a full recovery because they behave as if they are disabled. Medical opinion used to counsel such patients to take it easy, but now recognizes that heart patients need to reclaim as much of their former activity as possible. In the same way, the after-effects of physical injury can restrict your activity unless you use exercise and physiotherapy to regain as full a range of movement as possible.

Robert Lewin, Professor of Rehabilitation at Hull University, has a heart disease rehabilitation programme that is used in over 80 National Health Service hospitals.[2] It is designed primarily to change the way patients think about their disease. He reports that 80 per cent of heart attack patents attribute their illness to factors they feel they cannot change, such as worry, stress and overwork. These patients do not believe they are in control of their lives. Such beliefs cause further anxiety and depression in a vicious downwards spiral, for depression doubles the risk of premature death. It may be that you make as full a recovery as you believe you will.

THE BELIEFS OF MEDICINE

The operating principles of the current Western model of medical treatment:

1 Disease is a pathological process where the human body goes beyond normal biologically defined measures.
   It can be caused by too much of something (e.g. ultraviolet light, cholesterol).
   It can be caused by too little of something (e.g. vitamins, minerals, insulin).
   It can be caused by something that is intrinsically damaging (bacteria, viruses, radiation).

2 All illness has a biological cause.

3 Illness and disease are located in the patient's body.

4 The initial cause of an illness usually comes from outside the patient's body.

4 Treatment is by physical intervention (e.g. surgery, drugs) to get rid of or reduce whatever is causing the illness or disease.

5 It is possible by medical research to find a cure for all the diseases and illness that flesh is heir to.

2 Kent, Anne, 'Hope for a cure', *The Sunday Times*, 19 November 1995

6 Doctors know about disease. They are the experts. Patients
   do not know.

7 Doctors deal with disease and illness. Patients are people
   with disease and illness. Therefore doctors deal with people.

These are narrow but very widespread beliefs. If they are to change
and widen, we need to become aware of the consequences
they have and how we think about health and what we do if we
become ill.

EXPLORING BELIEFS ABOUT HEALTH

**How would you complete the following sentences? What does this
tell you about your beliefs?**

> **Being healthy means...**
> **If I am healthy then I can...**
> **Being completely healthy would mean changing...**
> **If I were to take charge of my own health it would mean...**
> **When I am sick, it means that...**
>
> **The following things stop me being healthy...**
> **The following things help me to be healthy...**

**Now take the answers to the last two questions and reverse them.
Think of how those things that you put as barriers to health could
actually help you to become more healthy.**
    **Then think of reasons why those things that you initially wrote
as helping you to be healthy could actually prevent you.**

**Here are some limiting beliefs about health, paired with the oppo-
site supporting belief. Complete them both.**
    Which is true for you?
    Which would you like to be true for you?
    A great deal depends on what being healthy means to you.

> **I do not deserve to be healthy because...**
> **I deserve to be healthy because...**

I may not regain my health because...
I will regain my health because...

It is wrong to want to be healthy because...
It is right to want to be healthy because...

It is not possible for me to be fully healthy because...
It is possible for me to be fully healthy because...

Being healthy is unrealistic because...
Being healthy is realistic because...

When you are free to define health for yourself, are there any facts that mean you have to believe the first sentence in these pairs rather than the second sentence?

Here are some prevalent beliefs. What do you think of them? Are there any you believe but would rather not?

When I get a headache it is best to take a pill.
Indigestion is best settled with an antacid.
Doctors should be obeyed.
I do not know enough about my body to take control of my health.
Illness is inevitable.
Aches and pains are part of growing older.
The more medicine I take, the healthier I am.
Childbirth is dangerous and needs to be medically managed in hospital.
I cannot get rid of pain without some sort of medical treatment.
I am responsible for my illnesses.
If a germ has got your name on it, there is nothing you can do.
I have very little influence on my health.
My health is determined by my hereditary – I am lucky or not.
Medicine ought to be left to the professionals.
To be really healthy I would have to give up all those things I enjoy.
Doctors are useless.
You should bear your pain and not complain.

If I have had a health problem for years, it will take years to resolve.
Changing is hard.
Once you reach age ... [fill in the gap] your health is bound to deteriorate.
I cannot control my feelings.
People are innately healthy or not.

Finally, what do you believe about being ill?
How do you know when you are ill?
What does illness mean to you?
How many of the following would mean that you were ill?
Are there any you would add to the list?

I have pain.
I am unhappy.
I am tired.
I feel weak.
I do not want to eat.
I do not feel like being with people.
I have to go to bed during the day.
I cannot think clearly.
I don't want to get out of bed in the morning.
I can't work.
People tell me I am ill.
A doctor says I am ill.
I vomit.
I have a temperature.
I have to see a doctor.
I feel anxious and upset.
I can't do those things I enjoy doing.
I do not know what is wrong with me.

What does injury mean to you?
How many of the following mean that you are injured and are there any you would add to the list?

I cannot walk.
I cannot play sports.
I have to go to hospital.
I have broken bones.

I am in pain.
It does not heal within a certain amount of time.
I have to see a doctor.
There is a bruise.
I have to stay in bed.
I lose blood.
I cannot use some part of my body as I normally do.

You can put this material on beliefs into practice right now.

Think of an area of health where you are not getting what you want.
Write an explanation of why you are not getting what you want.
What does this tell you about your beliefs about your health?
What beliefs would you have to change to increase the chance of getting what you want?
How much of your explanation would an impartial observer agree with?
Can you separate your beliefs from facts?

All beliefs have consequences regardless of their truth because we act on them. Beliefs are shown by what you do, not what you say. They also have biochemical consequences in our bodies. Beliefs can be toxic – our bodies bear the wear and tear of our beliefs. As we have seen, hostility, depression and feeling helpless all stem from beliefs about ourselves and the world and all are dangerous to health. Many beliefs about health presuppose, although this is never stated, that we are helpless in the face of attacks from marauding germs.

The lists above are one way of exploring your beliefs about your health: what is possible; where you believe your part ends and the doctor's begins. You might wonder about the wider implications. For example, an aspirin will probably stop the pain of the headache, but will not stop the muscle tension that may have caused it. You have blocked the signal that tells you that something is wrong.

TRUE OR FALSE?

How many of these statements do you think have been confirmed by medical research?

1   The single factor most likely to lead to a heart attack in American adults is chronic hostility in relationships.
2   People can have asthma attacks from being near artificial flowers.
3   Keeping a diary of your feelings about important life events gives a measurable positive effect on your immune system.
4   Those men who do volunteer work at least once a week have a death rate of half those who do not.
5   The pain relievers that we produce in our bodies – the endorphins and enkephalins – are 10 times as powerful as morphine.
6   Watching tropical fish swimming in an aquarium lowers blood pressure and heart rate.
7   People have been known to adjust their eyesight to nearsighted, farsighted or normal, changing the eye's curvature very quickly so that an optician would write a different lens prescription.

You might have guessed all these have been confirmed by research except for 5. (Our natural painkillers are over 100 times as strong as morphine.)[3]

Hostility has been found to be more important in the development of heart attacks than any dietary or environmental influence.[4] The studies do not say that anger is always bad. What literally 'breaks your heart' is hostility as a way of life – where people and events are seen as personal threats, and you react with constant defensiveness and anxiety about keeping what is yours, as if others are going to take it. Certain beliefs are necessary to act in this way.

People can have asthma attacks from artificial flowers – as long as they believe the flowers are real.[5] Our immune system responds not to reality, but what we think and believe is real. This reinforces the message that by changing your perceptions, you can change your immune system response.

Keeping a diary has been shown to have health benefits. Psychologist James Pennebaker studied a group of students who

3   Ornstein, R., and Sobel, D., *The Healing Brain*, Simon and Schuster, 1987
4   Williams, R., 'Curing Type A: the trusting heart', *Psychology Today*, January–February 1989, 36–42
5   Mackenzie, J., 'The production of the so-called "rose cold" by means of an artificial rose', *American Journal of Medical Science* 9 (1886), 45–57
    also see Ader, R. (ed.), *Psychoneuroimmunology*, Academic Press, 1981

had been asked to write down their feelings about upsetting and traumatic experiences. A control group of students wrote about trivial events. The study was conducted over four days. The students who had confided the upsetting events in their diary had fewer visits to the doctor in the following six months. Pennebaker also found those students had improved immune system function six weeks after the end of the four-day study.[6] Even confiding in a diary seems good for the soul. Perhaps it helps by putting the traumas outside yourself, so you can dissociate from them, learn from them and view them more dispassionately.

Volunteer work is one way of going beyond yourself and connecting with others. It is the opposite of self-absorbed hostility. A large health study in Tecumsah, Michigan, followed nearly 3,000 people for 10 years. The death rate of men who did regular volunteer work was two and a half times lower than those who did no such work.[7]

If you have ever gazed at tropical fish in an aquarium, you will know the kind of drifting, relaxing state that they induce. Their graceful movements are flowing and languid. There is something beautiful and engaging about looking at life that abstract patterns cannot imitate. In studies of people with high blood pressure, watching tropical fish in an aquarium was found to lower blood pressure. Watching an empty aquarium raised their blood pressure and they became bored.[8] We doubt if you need to invest in a tropical aquarium to get the effect. The languid, relaxed state it induces is the benefit.

The eyesight changes have been found in people with multiple personality disorders (MPD). Such people seem to house several different personalities which will appear at different times. Each

6 Pennebaker, J., Hughes, C., and O'Heeron, R., 'The psychophysiology of confession: linking inhibitory and psychosomatic processes', *Journal of Personality and Social Psychology* 52 (4) (1987), 663–76
    also see Pennebaker, J., 'Confiding traumatic experiences and health' in Fisher, S., and Reason, J. (eds), *Handbook of Life Stress: Cognition and health*, John Wiley and Sons, 1988
7 House, J., Robbins, C., and Metzner, H., 'The association of social relationships and activities with mortality', *American Journal of Epidemiology* 116 (1982), 123–40
8 Katcher, A. *et al.*, 'The physiological consequences of interaction with the living environment' in Katcher, A., and Beck, A. (eds), *New Perspectives on our Lives with Animal Companions*, University of Pennsylvania Press, 1983

personality may think it is the only one and deny the existence of the others. MPD is nearly always the result of childhood trauma where one or more parts of the person become completely dissociated from the rest. One personality can have good vision while another may be shortsighted.[9] This means that eyesight cannot be fixed or all the personalities, sharing the same eyes, would have the same vision.

BELIEFS ARE LIKE POSSESSIONS

We talk about beliefs as if they were possessions. The language is particularly revealing. We 'have' beliefs. We may 'adopt' or 'acquire' them and we can 'inherit' them. We say people 'hold' beliefs and even 'cling to' them. When we give them up, we 'disown' them, 'discard' them, 'abandon' or 'lose' them.

If beliefs are possessions, we may be possessive. Some could be precious heirlooms, others more everyday objects. Some we put on public view, others are too valuable to be shown to all and sundry. We choose them in many ways and, like furniture or decorations, we choose them so they do not clash. Some beliefs we may like, but they would not 'fit' with the decor. If you were to think of beliefs as possessions that you could choose and discard at will rather than at random, how would you decorate and furnish your inner world?

USEFUL BELIEFS

You may look twice at this heading if you have been used to thinking of beliefs as simply either true or false. NLP suggests that it is useful to replace the idea of beliefs with the idea of 'presuppositions'. Presuppositions are principles of action. They are like beliefs, but you choose them. You do not know if they are true or not, but you act as if they are true and pay attention to the results you get. This is quite reasonable because we never really know if

9 Goleman, D., 'Probing the enigma of multiple personality', *The New York Times*, 28 June 1988

what we believe is true – but the consequences are real enough.

You keep presuppositions for as long as you get results that enhance your health and well-being. You change and modify them when you do not get results you like. Because beliefs act as self-fulfilling prophecies, acting as if they are true makes it more likely you will get results in accord with them.

What presuppositions would you like to have about health and illness? Which ones would be positive and supportive for you?

We would like to give some suggestions:

- *Your body is naturally healthy.*
  The major activity of the body is to survive and repair itself. It heals itself naturally. Every time we cut ourselves, we see healing at work to repair the injury. The skin heals, the wound is repaired. Even in the worst of circumstances against all odds, the body will try to heal and survive. It can heal itself of any illness with the necessary work. The problem is to know what the necessary work is. Illness and disease are states where the body is off balance. Healing is the return to health, a return to balance. This also means you can trust your body. The messages it gives you in the form of pain or illness are signals that something is wrong. It needs attention. The body is not a capricious enemy that will let you down given the slightest opportunity.

- *You can learn from every illness.*
  Appreciate your body's marvellous ability to heal and think back to what happened before you were ill. What factors do you think contributed to the illness? Some factors will be outside your control. But there will be some within your control that you will be able to change.

- *Mind and body are one system – the same self.*
  What you think affects your body and what you do with your body affects your thoughts. This gives you control and influence. You can avoid those thoughts that harm your health and cultivate those that enhance it.

- *Symptoms are signals.*
  Find out what the signal means, rather than immediately trying to remove it. When you pay attention to what your body is

telling you, you are pacing yourself, getting to know deeper
levels of yourself.

THE SUBMODALITIES OF BELIEFS

Beliefs have a submodality structure. We represent those things we
believe in a different way from those we doubt or disbelieve.

**Think of something you believe. Nothing contentious. Something
banal like the sun will rise tomorrow or a country that you have never
visited really does exist. Now, as you think of that, notice the qualities of the picture you have. Write down the submodality structure of
the belief from the list of submodalities on page 50. Pay particular
attention to the size and clarity of the picture and where it seems to
be in your visual field. The actual content of the picture is not relevant. If a submodality on the list does not make sense to you or does
not apply, just leave it out. If you notice a quality of the picture or
sound that is not listed, write that down as well.**

**Then think of something you doubt. Make it obvious, for exam-
ple, your shoe will turn into an elephant. Look at the picture you
have of this. The content does not matter. Check the submodalities of this doubt by going through the lists on page 50 as you did
for the belief. They will differ in an interesting way from the
submodalities of the belief.**

**Do not mistake the feeling of certainty that you have about the
belief for a submodality. The feeling of certainty is a reaction to
the submodality structure and not part of it. Similarly, the feeling
of doubt you experience is not part of the submodalities, but your
reaction to the way you have represented it.**

CHANGING BELIEFS

You may have discovered some beliefs you want to change. Do you
believe that you can change your beliefs? You must have done so in
the past or you would still believe everything you did as a child. We
all have a personal mausoleum full of relics of discarded beliefs.

You cannot just drop beliefs, that would leave a black hole in
your mental universe. You have to replace them with another
belief that you prefer to have. There are many formal techniques

for working with and changing beliefs in NLP.[10]

When you find a belief that you would like to change, ask yourself some questions:

What is this belief doing for my health?
Does it enhance my health?
What am I doing based on this belief that injures my health?
How does this belief help me?

You may start to feel some doubt about the old belief. Is it true under all circumstances? Does everyone believe it? If not, why not? Start to notice situations that do not fit well with your old belief. Think of all the beliefs about health that have come and gone in the medical literature over the last decade. Medical science can and has been wrong. Take a visit to your own mausoleum of old beliefs. What do you find there?

Then ask yourself:

What would I rather believe?
How will my health be better with this new belief?
How might my health be worse with this new belief?
What is the best thing that could happen based on my old belief?
What is the best thing that could happen based on my new belief?
What might stop me adopting this new belief?
What is there in my life that already fits this new belief?
How will my new belief fit with my sense of myself?

You will find that not only is it possible to change a belief, but easy too, provided:

• You replace it with a belief that you prefer.
• You keep the benefits the old belief gave you.
• The new belief is in harmony with your sense of self.

Then act on the new belief!

10   Dilts, R., *Changing Belief Systems with NLP*, Meta Publications, 1990
     also Dilts, R., Hallbom, T., and Smith, S., *Beliefs: Pathways to health and well-being*, Metamorphous Press, 1990

FOOD FOR THOUGHT

God cures, and the doctor sends the bill.

Mark Twain

It ain't so much the things we don't know that get us into trouble. It's the things we know that just ain't so.

Artemus Ward

Physicians pour drugs of which they know little, to cure diseases of which they know less, into humans of which they know nothing.

Voltaire

5

THE PLACEBO EFFECT

Medicine uses the enormous power of beliefs by another name. Doctors prescribe beliefs in the form of placebos. A placebo is often narrowly defined as 'an inert substance that has its effect by virtue of the patients' expectations, having no direct effect on the condition for which is prescribed'. But as we shall see, it is hard to separate direct and indirect effects, and a placebo can be a substance, a procedure or a form of words. All that is necessary is that it mobilizes the patient's beliefs and thus their immune system. This chapter is about the placebo effect – how beliefs, expectations and trust, in many different guises, can heal illness and influence our health and immune system.

THE MOST TESTED DRUG

Which drug has been subject to the greatest number of rigorous clinical tests? The placebo. It is also the most used drug in the history of medicine. Placebos are so well researched because all drugs are subject to a double blind test to gauge their potency and side-effects. A group of patients is given either the drug under test or an inert substance – the placebo. 'Placebo' is often used synonymously with 'sugar pill'. The results are monitored. The test is called 'double blind' because neither the testers nor the patients know who receives the drug and who receives the placebo. The patients must not know because what they expect will affect the results. The researchers must not know because their own beliefs and expectations influence the patients, who are apt to pick up clues from voice tone and body language. Beliefs are infectious.

The placebo is a blank prescription on which we write our beliefs and expectations, a blank cheque for health. It may be an inert pill. It may be surgery. It may be a potent drug which has no direct effect on the illness for which it is prescribed. The placebo effect translates our beliefs about our treatment directly and sometimes surprisingly into material reality. It shows our natural healing powers at work. It directly contradicts the idea that illness is only in the body.

THE NEXT PENICILLIN?

Although placebos are effective in a large percentage of cases, medical training and medical textbooks pay them scant attention. They are treated as an embarrassing curiosity on the fringes of medicine, but really they belong at the centre. They are in an analogous position to penicillin. Penicillin was the first antibiotic and one of the most useful drugs ever discovered. Researchers trying to cultivate bacteria were frustrated because the penicillin mould would also grow and contaminate the experiments. It was a nuisance because it killed the bacterial cultures. When researchers stopped trying to get rid of it and actually noticed what it was doing, they extracted the phenomenal drug from the mould and arguably transformed the practice of medicine. The mould was more important than the experiments it ruined.

The word 'placebo' is Latin for 'I will please' and may have originated from the idea that the patient became well to please the doctor or that the doctor gave something just to please the patient. In either case the treatment had no 'medical' value. Embedded in this definition is the belief that treatments can be divided into those that work by virtue of their biological efficiency and those that do not, and that healing and curing is brought about by treatments that have proven physiological effects on the patient's illness. This is precisely the belief that placebos call into question. Here are treatments that can and do cure every sort of illness in a high percentage of cases, sometimes miraculously, yet according to the traditional medical model should have no effect. What is going on?

THE PLACEBO

The Most Consistently Effective Pain Reliever

There have been many double blind studies on the efficiency of placebos in pain relief. On average, placebos are 55 per cent as effective in pain relief as morphine. In other words, the reduction in pain with the placebo is 55 per cent of the reduction in pain achieved by morphine.[1]

In a typical clinical situation 25 per cent of patients will not get relief from any medication, even morphine. About 40 per cent of patients will get considerable relief from morphine but little benefit from a placebo. About 35 per cent of all cases will receive as much relief from a placebo as from morphine.[2]

Placebos are also 59 per cent as efficient in relieving depression as the tricyclic psychotrophic drugs.[3]

A MOUSE IN MAY KEEPS THE DOCTOR AWAY

Medicine's success has relied on the placebo effect. The history of medicine is littered with treatments that could have had no direct effect on the illness for which they were prescribed, except to make it worse. A Roman prescription for a healthy life was to eat a live mouse at the beginning of each month (presumably on the grounds that nothing worse was likely to happen for the rest of the month). In Europe during the nineteenth century bleeding and purging were deemed essential. When these became discredited, doctors began to prescribe large quantities of opiates, alcohol and then cocaine. These are *active placebos* – powerful drugs that have profound physiological effects, but not on the illness for which

---

1 Evans, F., 'Expectancy, therapeutic instructions and the placebo response' in White, L., Tursky, B., and Schwartz, G. (eds), *Placebo: Theory, research and mechanism*, Guildford Press, 1985, pp.215–28
2 Evans, F., 'The placebo response in pain control', *Psychopharmacology Bulletin* 17 (2) (1981), 72–9
3 Morris, J., and Beck, A., 'The efficacy of antidepressant drugs', *Archives of General Psychiatry* 30 (1974), 667–74

they were prescribed. At least a sugar pill does you no harm.

We laugh at some of the quaint medical treatments of the past: bat's blood, ground crocodile teeth, hair from a skull. Yet they worked. Sometimes. And not due to their medicinal properties. What of modern prescriptions? Doctors prescribe a wide variety of active placebos. Antibiotics are prescribed for the common cold, despite the fact they have no effect at all on viral infections. Tonics and cough syrups have no direct effect on the illnesses they are prescribed for. Tranquillizers are the most widely prescribed modern placebo, too widely prescribed maybe. They can also be addictive. Tranquillizers are direct heirs to the opiates that were prescribed in the nineteenth century. A cynic would conclude that millions of pounds are wasted on such drugs because they are much more expensive than sugar pills.

SOME MYTHS ABOUT PLACEBOS

- *Only drugs can be placebos.*
  No. Anything that mobilizes a person's expectations and beliefs about health can act as a placebo, including surgery.

- *Placebos only work on psychological symptoms.*
  No. They work on a wide variety of illnesses, including arthritis, asthma, bleeding and obesity. They have a measurable physiological effect on the body. When placebos relieve pain, doctors sometimes conclude that the pain was imaginary, but there is no such thing as imaginary pain. Pain is real to the sufferer.

- *A placebo is an inert compound.*
  No. People have expectations about active drugs that may enhance or work against the drug's natural effects.

- *The placebo effect is evoked by deceiving people that they are receiving something that works when they are not.*
  No. Any treatment that enhances a person's expectations and sense of control can give the placebo response.

- *The placebo response is very weak.*
  No. The effect stimulates endorphins. These natural

painkillers are 100 times more powerful than morphine. Placebos can also neutralize the effect of many powerful drugs.

- *The placebo effect is always beneficial.*
  No. The placebo effect follows expectation and belief. When patients believe they are receiving a drug with unpleasant side-effects, they may get these side-effects with the placebo. For example, in a study of the drug Mephenesin, a placebo produced almost identical side-effects: sleeplessness, nausea and dizziness.[4]

- *Only hysterical, gullible or sensitive people respond to placebos.*
  No. There is no evidence that any personality type responds more strongly than another. Placebos work with every personality type.

- *Placebos necessarily involve deception.*
  No. There can be a placebo effect even when patients *know* they are receiving a sugar pill. In a study at Johns Hopkins Medical school, 15 patients who were attending a psychiatric outpatient clinic for anxiety were given sugar pills for one week. They were told openly that these were sugar pills and that they had been helpful to many people. Fourteen of the 15 patients reported their anxiety was significantly reduced. Nine attributed the benefits directly to the pills. Six were convinced the pills contained an active ingredient. Three reported side-effects of blurred vision and a dry mouth.[5]

PLACEBO SURGERY

Any form of treatment can evoke the placebo effect. In the 1950s a common surgical treatment of angina was to tie a ligature around the internal mammary artery that runs near the heart. Doctors argued that tying the artery would divert blood to the heart and the increased blood flow would help to relieve the pain of angina.

4 Wolf, S., 'The pharmacology of placebos', *Pharmacological Reviews* 11 (1959), 689–714
5 Park, L., and Covi, L., 'Nonblind placebo trial', *Archives of General Psychiatry* 12 (1965), 336–45

A controlled study was carried to see how much of the improvement might be due to a placebo effect.[6] The patients were told they were part of a study but were not told that some of them would not be receiving the operation. A number of sealed envelopes were prepared with instructions either to tie the artery or to do nothing. In the middle of each surgical operation, the surgeon would choose an envelope at random and carry out the instructions – a strange procedure for the surgeon. Seventeen patients took part in the study. Five of the eight patients who had the real operation reported that they felt very much better. And so did five of the nine patients who had the bogus operation.

A group of sceptics repeated the experiment. Neither the patients nor the doctor who assessed them knew who had the real operation. There was a marked improvement in 10 of the 13 who had the real operation and in all five who had the bogus operation.[7] The operation was formally discredited as a treatment for angina and is no longer performed. It was not risk free and had no effect on longevity. (A study such as this would not pass an ethics committee today.)

In Denmark 15 patients underwent an operation for Menière's disease – a inner ear disorder causing deafness and dizziness. Fifteen patients had a placebo operation. A three-year follow up of both groups showed that 10 in each group had almost complete relief from the symptoms.[8]

Even in straightforward operations with proven benefits, a good outcome does not depend solely on the surgeon's skill with the scalpel. Patients who are visited by the anaesthetist the night before, reassured and told what will happen, often need less anaesthetic the next day, do better in surgery, are discharged more quickly and have fewer post-operative complaints. The eminent surgeon J. Finney, who was Professor of Surgery for many years at John Hopkins Medical School stated publicly that he would not

6   Cobb, L., Thomas, G., Dillard, D., Merindino, K., and Bruce, R., 'An evaluation of internal-mammary artery ligation by a double blind technic', *New England Journal of Medicine* 260 (1959), 1115–18
7   Diamond, E., Kittle, C., and Crockett, J., 'Comparison of internal mammary artery ligation and sham operation for angina pectoris', *American Journal of Cardiology* 5 (1960), 484–86
8   Thomsen, J. *et al.*, 'Placebo effect in surgery for Menière's disease: three year follow-up', *Otolaryngology – Head and Neck Surgery* 91 (1983), 183

operate on any patient who expressed a fear that they would not survive the operation.[9]

There is also evidence that patients under anaesthesia can hear what the surgeons are saying about them. Under hypnosis, patients have recalled comments made about them in the operating theatre that have been subsequently verified by those present. When these comments are negative and cast doubt on their recovery, the patients are worried.[10] Some doctors have proposed hanging a sign in every operating theatre saying, 'Be careful, the patient is listening.'

STRONG MEDICINE

The placebo effect is very powerful. It can reverse the normal effect of a drug. In one study, where a woman was suffering from severe nausea, the drug that relieved it was syrup of ipecac – usually given to *induce* vomiting.[11] It worked because the doctors had told her that it was a new and 'powerful wonder drug' that would relieve her nausea. Her belief reversed the usual pharmacological drug action.

The placebo effect is not confined to minor illness. It can work with life-threatening diseases such as cancer. Consider the story of Mr Wright as reported by Dr Philip West, one of the physicians involved with the case.[12] Mr Wright was suffering from advanced cancer of the lymph nodes – a lymphosarcoma. He had huge tumours the size of oranges in his neck, armpit, groin and abdomen. He was near death; all the doctors could do was to give him pain-relieving medication. They held no hope, but Mr Wright did. He was sure that a new drug would soon be developed. When a new drug called Krebiozen was to be tested at the clinic where Mr Wright lay dying, he begged to be part of the trial. His wishes

9   Finney, J., 'Discussion of papers on shock', *Annals of Surgery* 100 (1934), 746

10 Cheek, D., and Rossi, E., *Mind Body Therapy*, Norton, 1988, pp.113–30

11 Wolf, S., 'Effects of suggestion and conditioning on the action of chemical agents in human subjects: the pharmacology of placebos', *Journal of Clinical Investigation* 1950 (29) (1959), 100–9

12 Klopfer, B., 'Psychological variables in human cancer', *Journal of Projective Techniques* 21 (1957), 331–40

prevailed, although strictly speaking, he should not have been included, for only patients with at least a three-month prognosis were eligible.

Mr Wright received three injections in the first week. Bedridden for weeks before, he was walking round the ward talking with the nurses two days after the first injection. The tumour masses shrank to half their original size. Within 10 days he was discharged from hospital. Where two weeks before he had been breathing through an oxygen mask, now he went flying in his private aeroplane at 12,000 feet. No one else who received the drug was any better. The clinical trials of Krebiozen continued but the reports were poor. It looked as if the drug was officially useless.

Mr Wright became depressed when he heard this and after two months of perfect health relapsed into his original state. The tumours grew back and once again he was close to death. The physician who was treating him gave him hope. He said that the clinical trials were poor because the original drug deteriorated on standing, but a 'new, super-refined double strength product is due to arrive tomorrow'. This was not true, but Mr Wright regained hope and waited with terrific anticipation for the 'new product'. With great dramatic effect, the doctor gave him the first injection of the 'double strength, fresh preparation'. What in fact the doctor injected was *water*.

Mr Wright recovered even more quickly this time. Soon he was back to his normal life, flying his aeroplane in good health. The water injections continued. After two months, the Krebiozen bubble burst. It was announced in the press that the American Medical Association had evaluated the trials and had come to the conclusion that Krebiozen was worthless in the treatment of cancer. A few days after this report Mr Wright was admitted to hospital gravely ill. His tumours had returned and he died two days later. This may be the only pure placebo experiment ever carried out by an MD on a cancer patient.

This is an extraordinary story. What made the difference was not the objective facts about the drug, but what Mr Wright believed – his subjective reality. NLP is very interested in stories like this. How was it possible? As far as we know Mr Wright's immune system was normal, so a normal immune system had simply worked miracles. Do we all have this potential to heal ourselves – and if so, how can we harness it?

Many doctors advise treating as many patients as possible with new drugs while they still have the power to heal. This is not as cynical as it sounds. New drugs give the best results when they are first introduced and enthusiasm is at its highest. As ardour for a drug fades, so does its effectiveness. When it is seen to be less effective than hoped, enthusiasm drops further. The drug has not changed, but the beliefs of patients and doctors have.

For example, in 1957 propoxyphene was marketed as a painkiller under the name of Darvon. It was widely prescribed as a safe and effective analgesic. Combinations with aspirin and other painkillers soon became more popular and by 1970 enthusiasm for Darvon began to wane. Heroin addicts started to inject it intravenously and doctors questioned whether it was really as good as the old drugs. Soon after, it was withdrawn. Doctors interpret diminishing returns as a sign that a drug was never as good as they thought instead of as a falling off due to the placebo effect weakening.

I SHALL NOT PLEASE

The placebo effect does not only appear conveniently for healing purposes. It is based on our expectations, our hopes and fears, and it seems sometimes we create what we fear. When placebos elicit undesirable side-effects, they are called 'nocebos', which means 'I shall not please'.

In a study at Queen Elizabeth's hospital in Birmingham, 400 patients were told to expect hair loss from the chemotherapy that they were undergoing. Over 100 patients received an inert pill instead of chemotherapy, yet still experienced hair loss.

The nocebo effect is enormously enhanced when other people confirm our fears. Here we enter the realm of crowd psychology. Fear seems more infectious than hope.

One example of the negative placebo effect on crowds occurred in an American football game at Monterey Park, California, in 1987.[13] Four people became ill for no apparent reason. The doctor in attendance discovered they had all consumed soft drinks bought from a dispensing machine under the stands. In case the machines had become contaminated in

13 Cited in Cousins, N., *The Healing Heart*, Norton, 1983

some way, it seemed the safest course of action was to make an announcement over the loudspeaker system warning the crowd not to use these machines because they might cause food poisoning.

The authorities had the best of intentions, but if they had foreseen what happened next they would have thought twice. People began fainting and being sick throughout the stands. Many fled the game. Nearly 200 people suddenly became so ill that they could not move and ambulances from five hospitals had to be called to take them for treatment. One hundred people were hospitalized.

An investigation quickly found that the soft drinks machine was entirely innocent. When *this* news was announced people recovered miraculously and the patients in hospital felt better and were discharged.

The crowd magnified the effect, but often fear is as compelling as hope. When we are afraid of being ill, the fear and the uncomfortable self-consciousness it produces can create illness out of nothing. A few years ago Joseph bought some bread rolls for lunch and was halfway through the third when his wife pointed out that there was mould on it. Joseph looked at the wrapping and realized the pack was well past its sell-by date and should not have been for sale. He lost his appetite abruptly and suddenly became very aware of his stomach. What had been a comfortable full feeling moments before now felt more sinister. Was he going to be sick? Ought he to make himself sick? What unknown horrors grow on mouldy bread? Fear is not good for the digestion, but the bread stayed down. Joseph spent the afternoon in a state of trepidation and only felt really safe 48 hours later.

THE DOCTOR IS PART OF THE TREATMENT

Trust in the physician is an essential part of the placebo effect. Pills, potions or surgery act as placebos, but from where do they get their authority? The physician.

Many of us go to the doctor just to talk – not for a written prescription necessarily, but a dose of relationship. The doctor is there to help the patient get well, sometimes simply by caring.

We respond to the totality of the treatment, not just drugs. We respond to how doctors talk, the messages they convey by their words and by their body language. When we are afraid or in pain, our senses are heightened. We look to extract meaning from the doctor's every nuance. We want to trust, we need to trust. We are more vulnerable to suggestion. A diagnosis of cancer, given bluntly, can be like a death sentence, a pronouncement of doom. It has the same effect as a curse.

Even in small matters, what doctors say influences what patients expect and therefore what they are likely to feel. Joseph was at the dentist recently and was having a filling without any injection to anaesthetize the nerve. The dentist said, 'You shouldn't feel any pain. Let me know if you do and I will stop immediately.' He meant to be reassuring. Joseph heard the whole sentence clearly, but one word stood out above all others: '...pain...' Suddenly he expected to feel pain and was on the lookout for it so he could tell the dentist to stop. He would have felt better if the dentist had said, 'You can be perfectly comfortable while I fill this tooth. If you are not, let me know and I will stop immediately.' This suggests '...be comfortable...' The same principle apples when someone says, 'This won't HURT.' Who are they trying to kid? Doctors prescribe expectations as well as treatment and we supply the reality – our reality.

There is an interesting study by K. Thomas, a general practitioner, which was reported in the *British Medical Journal* in 1987.[14] He took 200 patients for whom he could not make a specific diagnosis – they suffered from general symptoms such as headaches, coughs and tiredness – and divided them into two groups. To the first group he gave a positive consultation, a firm diagnosis and a strong reassurance that they would soon recover. He told the second group that he was not certain what was wrong with them, but to return if they were not better in a few days. Half the patients in each group were given a prescription.

At the end of two weeks, 64 per cent of the group who had the positive consultation were better. On the other hand, only 39 per cent of the other group were better. Having a prescription did not make very much difference. Fifty three per cent of those who were better had a prescription. Fifty per cent of those who had not received a prescription were better.

14 Thomas, K., 'General practice consultations: is there any point in being positive?' *British Medical Journal* 294 (1987), 1200–2

This very interesting study suggests two things. First, a positive consultation has a significant influence on patient recovery and in some cases is more powerful than the placebo effect of the actual medicine. Doctors can tell patients outright that they are getting inactive placebos – sugar pills – and the placebo response will still occur. It seems the patients pay more attention to what the doctor expresses with his voice tone and body language. Doctors have, of course, seen sugar pills produce extraordinary healing reactions. They know and believe that these have an effect. Perhaps it is this belief that the patients pick up for the placebo to work. Certainly no deception is necessary.

Secondly, we trust the treatment mainly because we trust the person giving it. Doctors have enormous power and prestige in Western culture. They are the heirs to a tradition of healing that goes back to the Stone Age. The other emotion behind any medical consultation is fear. The spectre of mortality hovers in every consulting room. In fact, doctors are generally suspicious of a calm and relaxed patient, it is so unusual. When we consult a doctor we catch a quick glimpse of the mystery of life and death. The doctor has knowledge and knowledge is power. The doctor can make the body befriend us again. When doctors prescribe they write from knowledge and power. But this authority is not enough. Rapport between doctor and patient is essential for really effective treatment. There will always be doctors who get on with their patients, who are popular and whose patients seem to recover faster with fewer complications. This effect comes not just from what they do, but who they are. In a sense, the doctor is a placebo. Many people feel better simply from having seen the doctor. They are reassured. They have an explanation for their illness and they expect to recover. Some never bother to take their prescription. A good doctor is one who is reassuring, one who treats the person as well as the symptom. If only the body needed treatment the placebo effect would not exist. Doctors who deal with patients need rapport skills. Doctors without them might be better off in a branch of medicine without contact with patients. Rapport heals.

One of the recurring themes in the NLP trainings that Ian conducts for doctors is their feeling that they do their best work with people they have rapport with. Rapport establishes a healing alliance, increases their professional satisfaction and reconnects them with their purpose for coming into the profession – they care about people.

It is particularly important to reassure and inspire trust in patients who are in hospital. The environment is impersonal, they are isolated from friends and family, and anxious about their illness. What sometimes happens is that doctors talk about the patients in front of them, as if they were not there, depersonalizing them and reducing them to their bodily symptoms. This can make the patient feel even more helpless and angry, and these feelings make their condition worse.

THE SUBMODALITIES OF PLACEBOS

Pills must *look* effective as well as have the desired effect or people will be put off taking them. How comfortable would you be taking a purple capsule for a headache?
What effect would you expect from these?

a small white pill
a large white pill
a small purple capsule
a black tablet
a red pill
a blue pill

Which would you expect to have a greater effect – a pill or a capsule?
Drug companies research the submodalities of their products, as well as the chemical composition. Many studies have found that the size, shape and colour of pills lead people to expect certain effects from them.[15]
A market research company in Manchester called Scantest spent two years testing consumer reactions to pills of different shapes, colours, sizes and hardness of finish in a study commissioned by Sandoz, the Swiss drug manufacturer. Here are some generalizations from the research. A pill should look like what it does. Blue pills tend to be perceived as sedatives, pink ones as stimulants. Larger pills are judged more effective than smaller ones

15 Blackwell, B., Bloomfield, S., and Buncher, C., 'Demonstration to medical students of placebo response and non drug factors', *Lancet* 1 (1972), 1279–82

and bitter ones stronger than sweet. Capsules are considered more potent than tablets, whatever their size. An injection is generally considered to be more powerful than either. People expect yellow or orange capsules to alter their mood, either as stimulants or depressants. 'Strange' colours such as black or lavender could be hallucinogenic (pop music has anchored the colour purple to psychedelics). Capsules or tablets that are grey or dark red are often judged to be sedatives.

Even brand names seem to have an effect. In one study of pain relief for headaches, 40 per cent of the group receiving unbranded placebos reported a reduction in pain. 50 per cent reported relief with branded placebos, 56 per cent with unbranded aspirin and 60 per cent with branded aspirin.[16] So aspirin was slightly more effective than a sugar pill in relieving headaches, but the effectiveness of each was enhanced by a familiar brand name.

THE PARADOX OF PLACEBOS

Doctors often feel ambivalent about placebos. They are caught in a bind of their own making, believing that healing is done solely by drugs or surgery that directly affects the body. They know a sugar pill does not directly affect an illness, so it is hard for them to congruently prescribe it. They also believe that a placebo can have a remarkable and unexplained healing effect, but for that to happen they must deceive the patient into thinking it is a potent drug.

This is only an apparent paradox. The placebo effect is a healing power we all have. The placebo is the excuse we have to use it. Any successful treatment must use our own healing powers.

Apart from a few instances, doctors always have a choice about the treatment they prescribe. There are many treatments available, both medical and surgical, and no treatment works all the time, including placebos. Our beliefs can enhance, cancel or reverse treatment. What is important is that the doctor is congruent about the prescribed treatment. When doctor and patient believe the treatment is likely to be effective, the patient improves

16 Branthwaite, A., and Cooper, P., 'Analgesic effect of branding in treatment of headaches', *British Medical Journal* 282 (1981), 1576–8

in about 70 per cent of cases,[17] even when the treatment is a placebo. Congruence heals.

The most successful treatment has four aspects:

the congruence of the doctor
the congruent belief of the patient
the rapport between doctor and patient
the direct physiological effect of the treatment

The last one is never enough by itself.

CONCLUSIONS

What medicine do we need to help us heal? The answer will be different for everyone. Medicine has always been pragmatic. Like NLP, it uses what works. In that sense they are allies. Medical treatment is never just mental or physical, it is shades of both, sometimes more of one, sometimes more of the other. Placebos act in that medical no man's land where physiology and belief work together and it is hard to spot where externally administered treatment ceases and the power of the human body-mind-spirit to heal itself begins. We respond to the meaning as well as the form of the treatment.

You have great power to heal and you do not know how you do it; nor is there a coherent medical explanation. But your congruence and belief in the treatment you take and the doctor who administers it is as important as the treatment itself; your attitude to it will significantly enhance or hinder it. When you believe that healing is a long and difficult process, and you might never get back to full health, then those are the instructions you are giving yourself. Give yourself some positive suggestions. Give others positive suggestions, too. Be congruent about the treatment you accept. Trust yourself. Healing is natural.

17 Roberts, H., 'The magnitude of non specific effects', paper presented at the Conference on Examining Research: Assumptions in Alternative Medical Systems, National Institutes of Health, Bethseda, 11–13 July 1994

FOOD FOR THOUGHT

Placebo: An inactive substance or preparation given to satisfy the patient's symbolic need for drug therapy and used in controlled studies to determine the efficacy of medicinal substances. Also a procedure with no intrinsic therapeutic value performed for such purposes.

Dorland's Illustrated Medical Dictionary, 26th edition, 1981

The frequency with which placebos were used varied inversely with the combined intelligence of the doctor and his patient.

R. Platt, 'Two essays on the practice of medicine',
Lancet 2 (1947), 305–7

The doctor who does not have a positive effect on his patients ought to become a pathologist or an anaesthetist. If the patient does not feel better for your consultation, you are in the wrong game.

J. Blau, 'Clinician and placebo', *Lancet* 1 (1985), 344

Why is it deceitful to give a placebo if a large element of modern therapeutics is no better than a placebo? Is the gullibility of a good hearted doctor preferable to (and more ethical than) the scepticism of one whose prescription is pharmacologically inert, when the results are the same?

'Shall I please?' Editorial, *Lancet* 2 (1983), 1465–6

One should treat as many patients as possible with a new drug while it still has the power to heal.

Sir William Osler

35% to 45% of all prescriptions are for substances that are incapable of having an effect on the condition for which they are prescribed.

S. Bok, 'The ethics of giving placebos',
Scientific American 3231 (5) (1974)

Three of the four most commonly prescribed drugs treat no specific illness.

H. Holman, 'The "excellence" deception in medicine',
Hospital Practice 11 (4) (1976)

6

THE IMMUNE SYSTEM – OUR PHYSIOLOGICAL IDENTITY

How does the body heal itself? How do beliefs and expectations work their medical magic? How do states like loneliness, hostility and depression destroy our health? How can positive states of love and compassion be healing? Medicine searches for explanations. Exactly how does it work?

Mind and body are one system. We experience this all the time. We know it every day when we imagine the taste of good food and salivate. We also know it when we imagine a disaster and we feel that familiar churning in the pit of our stomach. We experience it strongly when our bodies respond to sexual fantasies. And we confirm it when we think of those we love and our hearts beat faster and we feel loving and loved. Somehow thought becomes sensation. Thinking leads to action – and it makes no difference whether the thought has a basis in reality or not. Every one of us has probably experienced paralysing terror at one time in our lives – from a dream.

THE GOSSAMER WEB

Our thoughts have physical effects on all our major organs through three systems:

- the autonomic nervous system
- the endocrine system
- the immune system

The autonomic nervous system runs throughout our bodies like a gossamer web. It has two branches, one that energizes us and one that relaxes us. The sympathetic system is the energizing part, it puts us into a state of readiness to meet challenge or danger. The nerve endings secrete neurotransmitters that stimulate the adrenal glands to secrete the powerful hormones norepinephrine and epinephrine, which increase the heartbeat and breathing rate and influence our digestion through the acid secretion in our stomach. That anxious feeling in the pit of your stomach comes to you courtesy of the parasympathetic nervous system.

If the sympathetic system is the 'on' switch, the parasympathetic system is the 'off' switch. The parasympathetic nerve endings secrete other neurotransmitters that lower our pulse and breathing rate. Parasympathetic responses are comfort, relaxation and ultimately sleep. When we sit down, listen to music and lose ourselves in pleasant reverie, it is the parasympathetic system that relaxes our bodies.

Closely allied with the autonomic nervous system is the endocrine system, which is made up of a number of the organs that secrete hormones – substances that regulate our growth, activity level and sexuality. The endocrine system transmits our thoughts into real body feelings and actions. It also secretes hormones known as endorphins and enkephalins that seem to modulate our reactions to stress and pain, and affect our moods and appetite as well as some processes of learning and memory. The pituitary gland at the base of the brain is the controlling centre for the whole endocrine system. Our adrenal glands, which are located over our kidneys, secrete hormones known as corticosteroids and many of these act like the sympathetic nervous system and prepare our bodies for action.

The immune system is the third major system that has effects throughout our bodies. Its job is to keep us healthy by protecting us from antigens from the outside, such as bacteria and viruses, and from the inside, such as tumour cells.

The autonomic nervous system (including the brain), the endocrine system and the immune system are intertwined. They are like three springs of different coloured water bubbling into the same river, not three separate rivers. The river is the ebb and flow of our life and while we sometimes catch flashes of pure colour from each system, overall they are inseparable.

The three systems exchange information through neurotransmitters made from proteins called neuropeptides. They produce their effects by having exactly the right chemical structure to fit into a receptor on another cell, which can be a long way away from where they were produced. Their effects are specific. Over 60 different neuropeptides have been identified and we do not know how many there are in total.

The limbic system, the part of the brain that deals with our emotions, is the focal point for neuropeptide receptors.[1] The nervous system, immune system and endocrine system all make and receive neuropeptides and at any moment there may be many neuropeptides floating in the body waiting to attach to specific receptors. The link between the neuropeptides and their receptors is the biochemistry of the emotions.

Immune system cells have receptors for all the neuropeptides and they can produce the same type of neuropeptide hormones that were once believed only to be found in the brain.[2] The immune system listens to your emotions through its neuropeptide receptors; it sends signals to the brain via neurotransmitters and the brain influences the immune system in the same way. The brain actively monitors and reacts to immune responses.

There is an even more direct and surprising link between the immune system and the brain. Some immune system cells enter the brain and change to glial cells – a type of connective cell in the brain. Immune system cells can also produce a hormone (ACTH, adrenocorticotrophin) which stimulates the adrenal gland.[3]

The nervous system, endocrine system and immune system act together, translating our thoughts into physiology. Many effects of the autonomic nervous system and endocrine system are obvious and immediate. When you make a picture of someone you love, your heart beats faster. You get immediate feedback, so the connection is easy to make. The connection is not obvious with the immune system. We get no immediate feedback of the effect of our pictures and emotional states on the immune system, yet there must be an effect because the nervous system and the

1 Pert, C., Ruff, M., Weber, R., and Herkenham, M., 'Neuropeptides and their receptors: a psychosomatic network', *Journal of Immunology* 135 (2) (1985)
2 Blalock, E., Harbour-McMenamin, D., and Smith, E., 'Peptide hormones shaped by the neuroendocrine and immunologic systems', *Journal of Immunology* 135 (2) (1985), 858–61
3 Smith, E., and Blalock, E., *Journal of the Proceedings: National Academy of Science* 78 (1981) 7530

immune system pass on their messages in the same way with the same neuropeptides. The mechanisms are there for the immune system to affect and be affected by our thoughts and emotions.

It seems our mind and intelligence are not confined to the two and a half pound lump of greyish white matter between our ears – they are distributed throughout the entire body.

A fascinating experiment described in the *International Journal of Neuroscience*[4] hints at the possibilities of affecting the immune system though mental imagery. A group of students were taught self-hypnosis and visualization and given a description of the special functions of certain immune system cells. Then every student made up their own personal imagery for increasing the adherence of these cells. This part of the experiment was well designed. If the researchers had insisted on a standard imagery format, all they would have shown was the efficacy of that format to influence immune system cells. Everyone is different in the way they use imagery.

After two weeks, saliva and blood samples were tested for immune system cell functions and compared before and after the experiment. The only statistically significant change in the immune cells was their ability to stick to foreign objects.

DEFINING A SENSE OF SELF

The immune system is very complex, although the work it does can be summed up very simply: it looks after our identity on the physiological level. We think it is worth getting to know a little about how the immune system works, to appreciate the beauty and precision with which it protects us all our lives, and also to be able to build some clear mental perceptions you can work with to stay healthy. Knowledge is the beginning of appreciation, understanding and the possibility of influence.

The immune system is complicated and largely unknown territory despite the mass of research in recent years. Like the brain it is proving as complicated as our vanity hoped and our intellect feared. It is usually portrayed as a killing machine or an army – 'repelling' germs, 'fighting' infections and 'mobilizing' resources.

4   Hall, H. *et al.*, 'Voluntary modulation of neutrophil adhesiveness using a cyberphysiologic strategy', *International Journal of Neuroscience* 63 (1992), 287–97

This metaphor is useful up to a point. The immune system does indeed kill 'invading' germs, but it is far more than a private army roaming the bloodstream on the lookout for trouble. It works by recognizing what is us and what is not. It disposes of whatever it recognizes as not us, such as tumours, bacteria, viruses and blood transfusions of the wrong type. It does on the physiological level what we do psychologically from infancy onwards – establishes boundaries between self and others. It is very suggestive that health on the physiological level is all about having a clear sense of self.

The immune system is defined functionally – by what it does. It is not neatly separated from the rest of the body, but considered part of the whole body.

The immune system itself consists mainly of leukocytes, specialized cells that are carried in the blood. ('Leuko' means white and 'cyte' means cell.) A healthy adult has about a trillion white blood cells, that is, 7,000 per cubic millimetre of blood. These cells perform a number of diverse tasks. Some summon other cells to engage bacteria and viruses. Others mark out the bacteria and viruses to be destroyed, and some call off the action and carry away the debris.

The immune system has two methods for defending the body. The first is called 'cell-mediated immunity'. Specialized cells recognize what is not part of the body and dispose of it directly. The second is 'humoral immunity'. Different specialized cells manufacture antibodies – large molecules that are exactly designed to destroy specific antigens such as bacteria.

THE UNBALANCED SYSTEM

The immune system normally knows what to attack and what to leave alone. For example, it leaves alone the many bacteria living in our intestines that help us digest food. But what happens when it does not work smoothly?

When the immune system does not react strongly enough to outside antigens such as bacteria or viruses, we fall ill. However, sometimes the infection may so massive that the immune system reacts normally but still cannot cope.

When, on the other hand, the immune system reacts too strongly to an outside antigen, then the result is an allergy. There

Mind–body link and the immune system

will be inappropriately strong response to a substance that does not present a danger. This is like a very sensitive or hostile person who constantly overreacts to harmless remarks. The immune reaction is more dangerous than the outside antigen.

When the immune system underreacts to an internal antigen, a cancer may develop. Our cells are dividing millions of times every day of our lives, and it is more than likely that abnormal and potentially cancerous cells are being produced all the time. If the immune system is weakened, then the cancer cells may escape detection and increase to a point where they are hard to control.

The immune system may also attack part of ourselves by mistake. This surfaces as an autoimmune condition such as rheumatoid arthritis. Here, the immune system seems to attack the healthy tissue of the cartilage in the joints, resulting in fatigue, muscle stiffness and swollen joints that are difficult to move without pain.

THE SEVENTH SENSE

We have five senses and some would say intuition is a sixth sense. The immune system is part of our seventh sense – our sense of self.

The immune system has many characteristics of a sense organ. The eye senses light, the ear senses sound and the immune system senses self. The eye is sensitive to light. The signals from the retina at the back of the eye are fed to the brain. The brain decodes the information and projects the picture outwards into the external world. We see. The immune system senses self, feeds that information back to the brain by neurotransmitters and the result is health. Our sense of self is necessary to our survival. We can close our eyes consciously and block the sense of sight, but we cannot deliberately disable our immune system. In NLP terms:

The immune system is the representation system of self. A strong immune system may be the physiological equivalent of a strong sense of self.

Anything that increases your sense of self is likely to strengthen your immune system. Anything that weakens your sense of self may weaken your immune system. NLP is about building a strong sense of self – becoming more self-aware by paying attention and being curious about your own experience in a non-judgmental way. By pacing yourself, you become less divided, more relaxed and intuitive, more congruent and in harmony. Being aware of your emotional states and building resource anchors starts to break the cause–effect links. So you are no longer the victim of events; you have more choice and control over your experience. You get to choose how you react rather than just responding like a jack in the box.

When we speak of the sense of self, this does not mean self as opposed to others. We are shaped by our relationships and our social relationships help define our sense of self. Therefore anything that strengthens our social support nurtures our health and vice versa. Depression, bereavement,[5] poor social connections and loneliness all weaken our sense of self and so are likely to lead to illness. When people lose close friends or spouses they often say it is as if a part of them had died. They have lost part of their sense of self.

It is ironic that illness forces you to take some time just for yourself, but not in a way that you would choose. So illness is not so much a sign of weakness as a signal to rebalance. We are never perfect, life is a balance between who we are and who we are becoming.

If the immune system is the representational system for yourself, then you can strengthen it by becoming more sensitive to your body by using your senses. Our bodily feelings are the music of the physical self. This does not mean developing an obsessive preoccupation with the body or becoming a hypochondriac. It means paying attention to your body directly and acting on the signals. Sometimes those signals will say, 'Slow down, you are working too hard.' Illness is the last stage, when the more subtle signals have been ignored. The body says, 'OK, let's see you ignore THIS!'

You can start to develop this awareness now. Become aware of your body. How are you sitting? What parts of your body are uncomfortable and need to be moved? Finding your baseline state will already have made you more aware of your body. It is ironic that we may spend a great deal of time developing some senses, yet neglect our sense of self which has such an effect on our health.

5   Schleifer, S., Keller, S., Camertino, J. *et al.*, 'Suppression of lymphocyte stimulation following bereavement', *Journal of the American Medical Society* 250 (3) (1983), 374–7

ALLERGIES – PHOBIAS OF THE IMMUNE SYSTEM

An allergy is rather like a phobia of the immune system. A person with a phobia of spiders, for example, will have a violent unreasoning response to seeing a spider or even imagining one. Logical thought does not help. They know that the spider is not a threat, yet to touch it is intolerable. An allergy is when the immune system reacts likewise – say, to cats, house dust or grass pollen. These are not threats; the immune system makes a mistake. Typical allergy symptoms include watery eyes, perhaps sneezing, a runny nose, shortness of breath or a rash. Like phobias, allergies often begin in childhood from a bad experience with the allergen and the reaction follows the person through life.

Asthma is one of the most dangerous allergies. Here the body reacts by constricting the bronchial tubes, which leads to difficulty in breathing. The trigger may be small, but the reaction can be very serious, even life-threatening. Asthma is not well understood medically. It may be caused by many different allergens and emotional stress also plays a part. The intensity and frequency of the attacks vary, and some people are lucky enough to be able to leave them behind in childhood.

Jorgen and Hanne Lund carried out a year's research study in Denmark on the psychological aspects of asthma and the influence of NLP therapy.[6] There were two groups of patients in the study, 30 in the intervention group, who received NLP therapy, and 16 in the study group. Both groups were taught to monitor their lung function and adjust their medication, giving them a sense of control and making them aware of limiting beliefs and the influence on their health.

At the start of the research, not all patients were convinced of the value of the therapy. Some dismissed the idea and others focused on the medical interventions. Both groups became more aware of how they perceived and reacted towards environmental stress. They started to use their symptoms as a signal that they were under stress and this increased their sense of control.

After a year both groups showed more stable lung function, but the intervention group showed greater improvement. Lung

6 Lund, J. and H., 'Asthma management', a qualitative research study presented at the Congress of the European Respiratory Society, October 1994

capacity of adult asthmatics tends to decrease by about 50ml per year and so it was in the control group. In the intervention group lung capacity *increased* by four times that amount – 200ml. The rate of hospital admission and severe asthmatic attacks was also greatly reduced in the intervention group.

Allergies are often triggered by anchors. In one experiment a doctor took into hospital a group of children who developed asthma attacks when they inhaled air that contained house dust. The researchers took dust from the homes of each of the children and sprayed it into the air of the hospital rooms. Nineteen of the 20 children had no reaction.

Alternatively, an allergen does not have to be physically present – it is possible to have the allergic response simply by thinking about it. There is hope here. If we can influence the immune system in one way to give the allergic response without the allergen being present, it must be possible to influence it the other way to heal the allergy.

NLP AND HEALING ALLERGIES

NLP has evolved a procedure for dealing with allergies. It works best where the person is allergic to a specific, easily identifiable substance. The method was developed by Robert Dilts, Tim Hallbom and Suzi Smith.[7]

First a warning. Allergies can be extremely dangerous, even life-threatening. These methods are not intended to supplant medical treatment but to work with it. When in doubt, leave alone.

The NLP allergy treatment re-anchors the immune system, breaking the link between stimulus (the allergen) and response (the allergic reaction). We will describe the procedure as if you were helping another person.

The first step is to build rapport. Acknowledge the other person's experience. The two of you are in partnership to change the allergic response.

Then begin by setting up an anchor for comfort and safety. Ask the person to think back to a pleasant situation where they were

7 Dilts, R., Hallbom, T., and Smith, S., *Beliefs: Pathways to health and well-being,* Metamorphous Press, 1990

very relaxed. Help them find a state that is not connected to the allergic response. When you can see from their face and breathing that they are relaxed, lightly touch their arm with your hand at a specific point. This is a tactile anchor for that state. Tell them that when they feel this touch, it will remind them to go back into this relaxed state and assure them that they can go to this at any time during the procedure.

Break state by distracting their attention. Now touch them again in the same place on the arm and watch to see if they go back to that pleasant, relaxed state. Check by asking them. Repeat the process until your touch reliably takes them to this relaxed state. Now you have anchored the relaxed state to your touch and ensured that if the person feels uncomfortable during the procedure, you can take them out to a pleasant, neutral state. This is the emergency 'bail out' anchor.

Next you want them to experience *just a little* of the allergic response, so you can see what it looks like. Ask them what it is like when they are in the presence of the allergen. Notice the change in their breathing, skin colour and particularly the moistness of the eyes. These are the first signs of an allergic response. In NLP, this is called 'calibrating' their response – you calibrate the allergic state by observing carefully what it looks like so you can recognize it again.

When you have seen the response, break state. Tell them a joke, distract their attention and get them to move their body.

The next step is to explain the immune system mistake. Tell them that the allergen is not dangerous, that their immune system is doing a fine job protecting them, but in response to the wrong stimulus. It can still safeguard them and does not need to react so violently to this particular substance. It has learned the response, now it will learn a new, more appropriate response. Start referring to the allergen as 'that substance' and not 'the allergen'. By giving it a new name, they will start to think about it in a new way. Tell them of the medical research into the immune system, how complex it is, how wonderfully it works and how it can learn from experience. Give them examples, if you can, of people who have lost their allergies.

The next step may take some time. What is the secondary gain from the allergy? Allergies do have benefits. They can determine what people eat, who they are friendly with and where they go on holiday. They can help them avoid certain types of social situation.

They can be used to control others or get attention. Perhaps an allergy to cigarette smoke is a way of preventing others smoking without the need to be assertive. The person suffering the allergy may organize events around the medical treatment they receive. When the allergy is healed, they may need to reorganize their life, make decisions, change their diet and get attention in different ways. Unless these issues are dealt with, the allergy is likely to stay in place.

Finish with a question like, 'If these issues of ... [diet, social situations, etc.] can be dealt with satisfactorily and your life is enriched, would you be willing to give up this allergy?' Listen for any doubt in their voice tone and only proceed when the person gives a congruent 'Yes.'

Next, find a substance to recondition the immune system. Ask the person to think of a substance that is very like the allergen, but does not give the allergic response. For example, a person may be allergic to bee stings but not ant stings, or to grass pollen but not plant pollen. Have the person associate fully into a memory when they were in contact with the harmless substance. Watch their breathing, eyes and skin colour carefully for any sign of the allergic response. If there is a response, find another substance.

When you have found a good example and the person is fully associated into a memory of being in contact with it, anchor that by touching the person on a specific place on their arm, different from the bail out anchor. This is the 'resource anchor'.

Now you are going to teach their immune system to respond to the former allergen in the same way as it responds to the harmless substance. The allergen is an anchor for the allergic response and you are replacing it with a new anchor for a neutral response. You must protect the person from the allergic response as you do this, so ask them to dissociate by seeing themselves behind a glass or plastic screen. Ask them to make the screen airtight and thick enough to keep the allergen out. Use the resource anchor by touching their arm and ask them to see themselves on the other side of the screen in a situation where they might meet the allergen. Ask them to gradually introduce the allergen into the scene behind the screen. You want them to see themselves behind a screen being perfectly comfortable in contact with the erstwhile allergen. Continue to hold the resource anchor. Watch the person carefully and stop if there is any sign of the allergic reaction.

When they can see themselves in the presence of the allergen without having the allergic response, you are almost finished. Still holding the anchor, gradually re-associate the person. Ask them to let the screen melt away, until it disappears. Then ask them to bring that picture of themselves being comfortable in the presence of the allergen behind the screen back into their own body so that they are back together in the present moment.

Finally, test. Remove the resource anchor and ask them to imagine themselves in the presence of the allergen now and notice if there is any of the old allergic response. Usually it has vanished or is greatly diminished.

Then have the person imagine coming into contact with the allergen in the future. This is the final test and is known as 'future pacing' in NLP. You mentally rehearse the person through the new response in an imagined future situation. Watch the person carefully for any signs of the old allergic response.

Best of all, test the allergy on the spot if this is realistic, appropriate and the other person congruently agrees. Take care if the former allergic reaction was very severe. Make safety your main consideration.

We have both used this allergy technique with success. One colleague of ours used the procedure on himself and cured himself of multiple allergies that used to incapacitate him for days at a time.

Here is a summary of the technique:

1 *Establish a 'bail out' anchor.*
This is a pleasant memory the person can go to if the procedure proves too challenging. Anchor this by a touch on the arm. Break state.

2 *Calibrate the signs of the allergy.*
Ask the person briefly to imagine being in the presence of the allergen. Calibrate to the signs of the allergy (moist eyes, skin colour change, breathing change), so both of you can recognize it again. Break state.

3 *Explain the immune system mistake.*
Explain how the process makes sense and is well grounded in medical research.

4 *Check for wider consequences.*
How would their life be different without the allergy? What are
the useful by-products of the allergy? Find a way to keep the
benefits without having the allergy. You may need to explore
new ways of coping with stressful situations.

5 *Find a resource.*
This should be as similar to the allergen as possible, but without giving the allergic response. Ask the person to imagine
being in contact with it as an associated memory. There should
be no trace of the allergic response. Create a resource anchor
for that state with a touch on the arm and hold that anchor
until the procedure is over.

6 *Have the person dissociate.*
The best way to do this is to ask them to see themselves on the
other side of a clear screen.

7 *Have the person imagine introducing the allergen.*
They gradually watch themselves on the other side of the
screen reacting normally to the allergen.

8 *Bring the person back to themselves.*
Have the person dismantle the screen and come back to
themselves.

9 *Test and future pace.*
Ask them to imagine being in contact with the allergen at
some time in the future and watch for any allergic reaction. If
possible and appropriate, really test the allergy with the
substance the person used to be allergic to. Take care!

This is a good example of the NLP approach to working with
health issues. NLP is very pragmatic. Rapport with the person you
are treating is essential. First you establish their present state, then
establish the desired state. Then you check out consequences of
the change. The next stage is to find a resource to help them get
from their present state to their desired state. Finally you test and
future pace. The procedure is successful when the person gets
their outcome. In practice you have enabled the person to influence their immune system through the power of their thoughts

and it is your words that have influenced their thoughts. Words are powerful, they shape the way we think about our health. How they do so is the subject of the next chapter.

FOOD FOR THOUGHT

It is more important to know what sort of patient has the disease than what disease the patient has.

Sir William Osler

God did not presumably put an opiate receptor in our brains so that we could eventually discover how to get high on opium.

Candace Pert

Some patients, though conscious that their condition is perilous, recover their health simply through their contentment with the goodness of the physician.

Hippocrates

The relationship between doctor and patient partakes of a peculiar intimacy. It presupposes on the part of the physician not only knowledge of his fellow man but sympathy. This aspect of the practice of medicine has been designated as the art. Yet I wonder whether it should not, more properly, be called the essence.

Warfield Longhope,
The Bulletin of the Johns Hopkins Hospital 50 (4) (1932)

METAPHORS OF HEALTH

To convey meaning we make comparisons, tell stories and share experience. NLP uses the word 'metaphor' for these comparisons, analogies and stories. 'Metaphor' comes from the Greek words meaning 'to carry across' and that itself is a metaphor. Metaphors are not true or false; they are ways of thinking, often useful, sometimes limiting.

A metaphor packs more meaning than a simple description. It is like a computer icon, springing to life when you click on it and giving a wealth of meaning, not just from what it is, but from what it makes possible and the limits it sets. Or think of metaphors as being like holograms: when you select a phrase that expresses the metaphor, the rest of the metaphor is implied, present but unsaid. It is like an iceberg below the surface.

Words themselves can be expanded to give metaphors about their meaning. The words 'health', 'whole', 'hale' and 'holy' all come from the same Anglo-Saxon root. 'Cure' comes from the same root as 'take care of'. 'Disease' is a lack of ease. 'Medicine' comes from the same Indo-European root as 'remedy', 'meditate' and 'measure'. All suggest a rebalancing.

MEDICINE AS WAR

Now we jump into the fray of existing health metaphors. The prevailing medical metaphor is not balance, but war. Health is described mostly as successful defence against constant attack from the outside. We use the vocabulary of warfare so naturally that we no longer think about it. The metaphor is powerful and pervasive. In its starkest terms you are under constant attack from 'alien invaders': germs are 'out there' trying to 'infiltrate' and cause illness. Constant vigilance is necessary. Tonics and vitamins can 'bolster the body's defences'. Recovery means 'battling' the illness, 'fighting' the disease. You may suffer from a sudden 'attack' or a 'chronic bout' of illness.

Look and listen to advertisements for the vast arsenal of drugs in the medical armoury. Some are described as 'painkillers', others are 'magic bullets'. Many of them 'fight' pain. When the war is over, the body repairs the 'ravages' of illness.

And our immune system? It must be our very own private army of security guards to fight infection. It 'patrols' the body, on the alert for intruders. It attacks and kills them and then carts away the debris. Health means continual alertness against unscrupulous germs – a body under siege. The 'fight against heart disease' and the 'war against cancer' are conducted with a huge defence budget to develop more and more sophisticated machinery and drugs to defeat the enemy, despite research that shows that we have a hand in creating these very conditions in ourselves. We have a foot in the enemy camp.

A battle cannot be won when you are fighting for both sides at once.

THE PREVAILING MEDICAL METAPHOR – HEALTH IS AN ARMED STRUGGLE

1 We are separate from the environment.

2 We are under attack from outside forces over which we have no control.

3 The body is under constant siege.

4 Maintaining health is a battle.

5 We win battles by killing the germs.

6 The body is amazingly complicated and only military experts (doctors) know about it.

7 The immune system is a killing machine.

8 Medical progress means better weapons and stronger drugs to fight disease.

9 While we may win the battles, in the end we always lose the war, because we die.

Metaphors are neither right nor wrong but they do have consequences. What are the consequences of acting as if the war metaphor is true? How does it influence our thinking? First it draws our attention to disease rather than health. When you are under siege you naturally look outwards to the enemy attack. So we look 'out there' rather than 'in here'. It encourages dependence on health professionals for answers, as if they control our own power for healing. We may become dissociated from our own health. Surgery is the most extreme form of dissociation from parts of our bodies. We literally separate from them. As a consequence of the war metaphor, we rely too much on the ability of medicine to repair the damage with drugs and surgery, and ignore what many fighters have considered to be the greatest skill in warfare – not fighting a battle unless you have to.

How can we make use of the metaphor of struggle in a different way? What would it be like to respond to illness as if it were a hostile takeover bid from another company? How might you scheme to defeat them? There might be better ways than killing their CEO and bombing their corporate headquarters.

The martial arts would be another way of thinking. What would it be like to maintain health gracefully, to use your opponents' own force to defeat them? Would you like to be a black belt in good health?

What do all great generals say about winning wars? Know your enemy. *The Art of War* is the oldest known military treatise in the world. In it Sun Tzu wrote:

If you know the army and know yourself, you need not fear the result of one hundred battles. If you know yourself but not the enemy, for every victory gained you will also suffer a defeat. If you know neither the enemy nor yourself, you will succumb in every battle.

So, still within the framework of the war metaphor, you can take command of your health. Know as much as possible about any illness you have, by reading, by asking questions, by paying attention to your body. Stop playing corporal and start acting like a general – it's your army that needs to be marshalled.

Illness can teach us a great deal. So often we try to batter it into submission with drugs without understanding it or our reaction to it. And there are consequences, just as in real life – the enemy comes back stronger and the drugs may damage your own territory, your own body.

HEALTH AS BALANCE – IT IS NOT UNHEALTHY TO BE ILL

Even though you can use the war metaphor to take command of your heath, we suggest it is out of date. Our knowledge about ourselves and our health makes it obsolete. We know appearances are deceptive and that our bodies are not something apart from the rest of the world. There is a constant intimate interchange of air and food. And atoms – at the end of this year, 98 per cent of the atoms in your body will be new. The outside layer of the skin replaces itself once a month. We grow a new stomach lining every 10 days and a new liver every two months. There is an intelligence at work in a body that constantly renews it and keeps it alive. Sitting beside a river, you see it has form and substance, even though you never see the same molecules of water twice, and it is the same with our bodies. No longer can we believe illness comes only from the outside. We know that our lifestyle, eating habits and thought patterns contribute to the current killers such as cancer and heart disease. We cannot completely defend ourselves against the world. We are part of it.

Health as balance is a useful metaphor and one we have used in earlier chapters. What are the consequences of this metaphor? We live in balance with the micro-organisms in the environment and an infection shows that the balance has been disturbed. Illness becomes a sign that we are out of balance and need to pay attention to ourselves. It need not be unhealthy to be ill. Illness can be a way of rebalancing ourselves, just as a temperature is a healthy sign, speeding up our immune system to heal more quickly. Many people somatize their experience – they become ill at a major turning-point in their lives. Their mental confusion is directly translated into physical illness. This can also be a healthy sign. Their old way of being was itself unbalanced and the symptoms of illness can be part of the transition.

HEALTH AS A BALANCE

1 We are part of the world.

2 Health is a balance of our way of being and the environment.

3 Illness indicates an imbalance.

4 Being ill can be healthy – it can rebalance us.

5 We know our own body best because we know it from the inside.

6 The body is constantly in relationship with micro-organisms. Some are beneficial, most are harmless and some can cause specific symptoms in susceptible hosts.

7 We stay healthy by taking care of ourselves and paying attention to the body's signals.

8 We have influence over our thoughts, emotions and environment.

9 The immune system is our physiological self. It knows what is us and what is not. It disposes of antigens to keep us whole.

10 Healing is a natural body process. We may need outside help to heal if we are greatly out of balance.

11 We are always healthy to some degree, just as we are always balanced in some way.

YOUR METAPHOR FOR HEALTH

Different metaphors open different ways of thinking. We are not trying to convince you there is a 'right' metaphor, but to encourage you to find one that works for you. You can decide which ones you live. They can be as simple or as complex as you wish.

First, become aware of those you have. What is your current health metaphor?

To find out, complete the following sentence:

Health is like...

Because...

How you think of health will influence what illness means to you and what you do when you are ill. Now complete this sentence:

Illness is like...

Because...

What do these metaphors tell you?
What do they allow?
What do they prohibit?
What else has to be true for these metaphors to hold?
What do both the metaphors have in common?

Just notice what your metaphors are. Do not try to change them yet.

When you have explored them, you may want different metaphors or you may want to enrich the ones you have.

Take a moment to think.

What do you want your health to be like?

I want my health to be like...

Because...

What would be the implications of this new metaphor?

How would you act differently if this new metaphor became true for you?

You can also change your illness metaphor:

I would prefer illness to be like... ˙

Because...

You may or may not immediately find a satisfying metaphor. If it is difficult, just answer with the first thing that comes into your head. For example:

Health is like ... a belly laugh.

Because ... it feels good.

Now, what is a belly laugh like?

A belly laugh is like ... a breath of fresh air.

Because ... it wakes me up.

You can carry on linking one metaphor to another until you have one that satisfies you. It is interesting to compare your old and new metaphor. Suppose your old metaphor for health was a struggle and your new one is drinking from a clear river. How do they connect? What do they have in common? Suppose you were to construct a story that took you from a struggle to drinking from a clear river. How would it go? How could a struggle be transformed into drinking from a clear river? This story can be as fantastic as you wish and may hold clues to your health. It is your journey from your present state to a desired state of health. Metaphors are not rational, but we think you will find that they have a logic of their own.

EMBODIED METAPHORS

What metaphor do you have for your body? Complete this sentence:

My body is like...

Because...

Just notice what it is and what the implications are. You can always change it if you wish.

What are the implications of this metaphor?
Is it different when you are well and when you are ill?
How do doctors fit into this metaphor?
Do you feel comfortable with it?
Is there a metaphor for your body that you prefer?

I want my body to be like...

Because...

If your body were like this, how would you see doctors and medical treatment differently?

Suppose your first metaphor was your body as a temple and you prefer your body to be like a stream of gold. How might a temple be transformed into a stream of gold? Again, the story of the journey from one to the other will give you ideas of the resources you need to change, and it will be in direct and poetic language.

CARS AND PLUMBING

What are the current medical metaphors for the body? Most imply it is mechanical and therefore dead. They show the body as a collection of parts rather than an organic whole. Medical treatments are influenced by the prevailing metaphor. The plumbing metaphor is a popular one – the body is like a vast processing plant, a collection of pipes carrying air or fluid. What do you do when plumbing goes wrong? You call in a plumber to fix it by cutting out and replacing bits of pipe or by flushing out the system and giving it a good clean. They will block some pipes and join others. This metaphor is limited but it can be useful. The coronary bypass operation is based on it. When the artery that brings blood to the heart muscle wall is blocked, it needs to be bypassed or replaced by veins taken from the lower leg. The operation can be beneficial, but for some patients it has no effect on longevity.

Sometimes the body is thought of as a car. 'Think of your body as a super automobile,' we read in one book. 'If you do not drive too fast for too long, and if you feed it the right fuel, give it periodic checkups, and maybe wash it occasionally, you will prevent problems before they climax in the transmission.' Of course you might also go on holiday to 'recharge your batteries'.

How do you maintain a plumbing system? How do you take care of a car? We are past the age of surgeons as butchers, but what do you think of surgeons as car mechanics and plumbers? Doctors as carpenters? TV repairmen? Huntsmen? Military strategists?

ORGAN LANGUAGE

Words express thoughts and our thoughts affect our bodies, our immune system and our health. What do our words tell us about how our thoughts are affecting our bodies?

Our words express our inner states and accurately reflect the way we think about our bodies. But we express ourselves not only with words but also with our bodies themselves. Words and body language are two ways of saying the same thing. Our bodies grow to express our habitual inner states with laughter lines or a furrowed brow. We say that people have a 'lived in' look.

We have a whole group of metaphors about our body called 'organ language' – they use parts of the body. Have you ever thought that someone is a 'pain in the neck'? It is an evocative phrase. Some people express that irritation another way. They get a *real* pain in the neck. The words can be prophetic: they express the thought and the thought affects the body. They are like self-inflicted curses.

We have been struck by how people keep repeating certain key phrases. We are not saying you have to avoid these types of phrases at all costs lest they come true. It is the chronic, unremitting, toxic metaphor that can do the damage. Words erode the body like waves against a cliff face. Being aware of organ language is the first step to making sure your body does not reflect the words in its own way.

Here are some typical bodily metaphors:

You are cramping my style.
This job is a stretch.
This worry is really eating me up.
This is driving me out of my mind.

You are getting under my skin.
I am going to burn out at this rate.
You make me sick.
She's eaten up with resentment.
You are getting on my nerves.
This work is killing me.
These kids are a pain in the neck.
You haven't the backbone for this.
This is a real headache.
That's spineless behaviour.
That turns my stomach.
Stand on your own two feet.
Don't use that as a crutch.
Don't be so limp.
That's a load off my chest.
They are twisting my arm on this one.
That is hard to swallow.
Stand up for yourself.
I just can't breathe freely in this atmosphere.
It's breaking my heart.
They are bleeding me dry.
This is back-breaking toil.
You make my blood boil.
Get it off your chest.
You get right up my nose.

DIAGNOSIS – KILL OR CURE

A diagnosis also shows the power of words. It is rather like a magical incantation – it names the unknown and takes away part of the mystery. It is the first step in the treatment. When doctors make a diagnosis, they are saying, yes, we know this condition, we have met it before, you are not alone. The words can act as a placebo.

A diagnosis can also be a curse. For many people the word 'cancer' is a death sentence. There is tremendous power in those six letters. Some people equate a diagnosis of cancer or AIDS with death, lose hope and cease to fight for life, so such a diagnosis can act as the ultimate negative placebo.

There is a powerful story told by Bernard Lown, Professor of Cardiology at Harvard, who was accompanying his chief on a clinical round. Lown's superior examined a middle-aged women who was suffering from congestive heart failure. Turning to his students, he said, 'This woman has TS,' and went on to the next patient. The women was immediately distressed. She told Lown that she believed that TS meant 'terminal situation' – a death sentence. Lown tried to reassure her that it meant 'Tricuspid Stenosis', which is a narrowing of the heart valve. She developed massive lung congestion and died the same day of heart failure.[1]

Diagnosis is the doctor's answer to the riddle of the patient's symptoms and sometimes doctors let the puzzle take precedence over the patient. The diagnosis can become an identity label in hospitals where doctors may refer to patients by their symptoms and not their names – 'the appendectomy in bed 10'. This is unfortunate and depersonalizes the patient at a time when they need all the individual identity strength they can get. If you have a medical condition, do not let the diagnosis become an identity. For example, people who have high blood pressure may start to think of themselves as 'hypertensives' and let the medical condition rule every aspect of their lives. This also happens to people who have diabetes. Diabetes does impose restrictions and difficulties, but there is a big difference between saying 'I am a person who has diabetes' and 'I am a diabetic.'

A diagnosis can create a new disease and so legitimize medical treatment. In 1976 an editorial in the *Lancet* actually asked the question 'Is grief an illness?' It went on to call for a more liberal supply of tranquillizers for the bereaved![2]

NOMINOMANIA

A medical label, especially if it is a complicated Latin name, gives an air of respectability that a condition may not deserve. The most impressive-sounding diagnosis may simply be a shorthand description of the condition in a dead language.

Medicine actually creates diseases. For example, in the nineteenth century, slaves in the southern states of America were thought to suffer from outbreaks of what was called 'drapetomania'.

---

1 Lown, B., 'Introduction' in Cousins, N., *The Healing Heart*, Norton, 1983, pp.11–29
2 'Is grief an illness?' Editorial, *Lancet* 2 (1976) 134

The main symptom of this 'disease' was an irresistible desire to run away – obviously inexplicable to the medical authorities at the time and therefore due to a pathological process. (*Drapeta* is the Latin for a fugitive slave.) Other 'symptoms' were being careless in their assigned tasks and breaking their tools. The use of psychiatric labels to detain and 'treat' dissidents in the former Soviet Union is a more recent example of medicine in the guise of political power. Perhaps doctors are prone to 'nominomania' – the irresistible desire to put labels on conditions.

Medical vocabulary is an insider language and often mystifying and confusing to those outside the profession. Every group has its jargon whose purpose is to attach simple labels to complex processes. (NLP is no exception.) But when medical jargon dissociates patients from their own physiology and confuses rather than enlightens, it should be dispensed with. Many doctors, to their credit, are excellent at explaining illness in easily understood terms. Paediatricians need this skill the most.

NAME THAT DISEASE!

Translate these impressive medical conditions into English.

You may find you suffer from some of these. This is perfectly normal.

thanatophobia
aptamosis
kynophobia
silurophobia
ergophobia
phobophobia
luculianism
bacchism
hedonia
iatrophobia
dysponesis
hypergelontotrophy

ANSWERS

thanatophobia – fear of death

aptamosis – the absence of sneezing or the inability to sneeze,

also known as 'asneezia' (some unfortunate 'asneezics' had to be cured of this 'complaint' by electroconvulsive therapy)[3]

kynophobia – fear of dogs

silurophobia – fear of cats

ergophobia – fear of work (epidemic on Monday mornings)

phobophobia – fear of fear (a condition of endless regress...)

luculianism – inclination to eat well

bacchism – inclination to drink well (epidemic on Saturday nights)

hedonia – defined in a recent book[4] as 'behavioural disturbance manifested by an uncontrollable urge to satisfy personal needs and to gain a pleasant feeling of satisfaction'. We think every healthy person needs this chronic condition, which no doubt includes both luculianism and bacchism.

iatrophobia – fear of doctors (which this list may have installed)

dysponesis – not feeling ill, but not feeling well either (the 'mustn't grumble' syndrome)

hypergelontotrophy – developing too great a sense of humour (not yet a medical condition, but beware!)

THE PURSUIT OF HEALTH

We become separated from health by the way we talk about it. Think about the phrase 'the pursuit of health' as a metaphor. It

3   Shukla, G., 'Asneezia: a hitherto unrecognised psychiatric symptom', *British Journal of Psychiatry* 147 (1985), 564–5

4   Sweet, W., Obrador, S., and Martin-Rodriguez, J. (eds), *Neurological Treatment in Psychiatry, Pain and Epilepsy*, University Park Press, 1977

implies that health is a quarry to be hunted. It must be fleeing, perhaps hand in hand with happiness. What does this suggest? That health is out of reach, that you are dissociated from it. You would only pursue something you did not have or did not realize you already possessed. It is possible to spend time pursuing health through diet and exercise and miss just how healthy you are and just how good you feel right now.

We talk about 'having' illnesses – a cold, high blood pressure or arthritis, say – but illness is not really a thing, it is a process. Making it into a noun is just a useful shorthand reference. Do not mistake the label for the activity. You cannot possess an illness, it is something you are *doing*. Many symptoms of common illnesses, such as a runny nose, sore throat and high temperature, uncomfortable as they feel, are your body's reaction to an antigen and an attempt to heal you.

Try this experiment. Think of an illness or a condition that you have had in the past or that you are suffering from now. We will take a cold as an example, but you can do this with any illness. Think of yourself when you had a cold. Look at the picture you have of that and any sounds and feelings that go with it. For most people this will be a still picture, fixed and unchanging. Now think, 'I am healing myself of the cold,' and notice how the picture springs to life. You are doing something. Thinking of illnesses as things tends to put you in the passive role. Now break state and put the thought of a cold in the past.

Illnesses and diseases are some of the few nouns for which we lack a verb. We say 'I have a cold' not 'I am colding.' It feels strange to 'verbify' illness, but it is more accurate.

Hypertension or high blood pressure is a good example. It is a complex interplay of forces in a person's body, not something they have, like blue eyes. We know how to raise our blood pressure at will – just think of an unpleasant or challenging experience. The stress of having your blood pressure taken by a doctor usually puts it higher than normal. In medical terms high blood pressure of unknown cause is termed 'essential hypertension'. But is it really essential or even necessary?

Some fascinating research has been done on high blood pressure and how it is affected by the simple act of speech. Talking for 30 seconds can cause blood pressure to rise by 50 per cent. The talking need not be stressful. Blood pressure simply mirrors human communication: it goes up when you speak and down when you are silent.[5] A graph of any person's blood pressure during a conversation would show exactly when they talked and when they listened. Furthermore, the higher a person's resting blood pressure, the more it rises when they speak. Rapid speech gives a greater rise than slow speech. Many hypertensive patients do not breathe freely when they speak, which also leads to an increase in blood pressure.

Blood pressure is a hidden form of communication. It is feed-back to yourself, responding to what you do, how you breathe and communicate with others. Patients are being taught to manage their blood pressure by recognizing their feelings, with-drawing from dialogue and social situations that are stressful, talking more slowly, breathing fully while talking and relaxing when necessary. They gain a measure of control. We think this is a beautiful example of a presumed fixed condition dissolving into a process, and in doing so, pointing towards some helpful actions.

MEDICAL METAPHORS

Medicine is not just a collection of treatment procedures, but also a way of understanding the world. It fits into the world view and mores of the society in which it is practised. Medicine is also prag-matic – it uses what works and discards what does not, despite resistance from people with a stake in the status quo. The danger for medicine is to become trapped in one 'correct' view of reality and demean or suppress alternative explanations. We do not toler-ate this in people, so why should professions be exempt?

Medicine is necessarily conservative. It plays safe because people's well-being and perhaps lives could be at stake. At the same time it needs to be humble; there are many instances where the existing medical establishment has been wrong in trying to uphold the received wisdom.

Allopathic medicine – the prevailing form of medicine in

5 Malinow, K., Lynch, J., Foreman, P., Friedmann, E., and Long, J., 'Automated blood pressure recording: the phenomenon of blood pressure elevations during speech', *Angiology* 33 (7) (1982), 474–9
   see also Lynch, J., 'The broken heart: the psychobiology of human contact' in Ornstein, R., and Swencionis, C. (eds), *The Healing Brain*, Guildford Press, 1990

Western society – is one system, grounded in one way of looking at the world. If we are faithful to medicine's pragmatic spirit, then we will be willing to look at other metaphors of health and illness, other systems of medicine. Homoeopathy, osteopathy, acupuncture, and Chinese medicine all have well developed philosophies and treatment procedures. They are all alternative metaphors for health and illness. They offer many kinds of prescriptions from familiar chemical interventions, perhaps in the form of herbs, to less obvious, but sometimes equally useful behavioural interventions such as to laugh more or to spend some time with children every day, for there is a wisdom in these activities that drugs cannot mimic.

Different systems have different metaphors. It is not a case of right or wrong. No system should be so arrogant as to claim the whole truth for itself (which has been the case with the more rigid apologists for allopathic medicine). Each system has its philosophy and basic metaphor and they all work for some people. No system has a monopoly of cures; all achieve some cures, including cases of advanced organic disease. We choose what we are prepared to believe in.

Your congruence and belief in the power of the system of medicine you use are just as important as the system itself. Be well informed. You may find different illnesses are best treated with different medical models. For example, we would not hesitate to have orthodox medical treatment for such problems as appendicitis, pneumonia and broken limbs. Once the crisis is passed, however, there may be other ways to speed the healing process, perhaps through acupuncture or homoeopathy.

On the other hand, modern medicine can offer little to alleviate back pain except drugs and operations to remove or reset parts of the spine. And two thirds of back pain sufferers who resort to surgery end up with more pain than before. But osteopathy, chiropractic, Alexander technique or Feldenkreis work would address what the sufferer had done (and probably is still doing) that puts them in pain, so they can learn to use their body differently, and properly conducted medical research has found consistently that acupuncture is effective for pain relief.[6]

Allopathic medicine can do little for the common cold.

6 In particular, the studies in the *British Medical Journal* 1 (6053) (1977), 67–70 and *Acta Anaesthesiology Scand,* 36 (6) (1992) 519–25

Homoeopathy and aromatherapy may well give better results. Chinese herbal medicines can give excellent results for chronic painful skin conditions such as eczema. Dietary factors may need to be taken into account. Steroids are often prescribed for serious eczema. These can have serious side-effects that include suppressing the immune system.

Joseph uses homoeopathic remedies for his colds and 'flu because they work (for him). The first time he took a homoeopathic remedy for a cold he swiftly recovered, and established an anchor for healing quickly and easily. Whether he recovered any more quickly than by doing nothing is uncertain. Homoeopathy has been shown consistently to give benefit in medically accepted, properly conducted, double blind tests,[7] but it still tends to be dismissed by a medical establishment that does not understand how it works. This makes no difference. We are equally ignorant of why some medically established drugs work.

For the last 10 years, Ian has had regular acupuncture. He did not start because of any specific illness, but because he was interested in its preventative as well as curative properties. Over the years, his experience is that he walks out of the acupuncture session feeling very well and constitutionally stronger.

Ian's experience is that acupuncture works. Joseph's experience is that homoeopathy works. Use what works for you – you do not have to justify it or be able to explain it. Trust your experience.

SECOND OPINION OR DIFFERENT METAPHOR?

Medicine is not an exact science and the second opinion is a useful and well established tradition. Doctors are human, they may make mistakes, or their advice may be coloured by what they have found successful and that may not be what works for you. They use procedures that *they* are congruent about, but that does not mean you have to be. It is wise to take different perspectives on something as important as your health and it is really important if you are contemplating surgery, for there may be other possibilities. No doctor can know them all.

When you have a health issue, why limit yourself to a second

7   Reilly, D., *Lancet*, 10 December 1994

opinion within the same metaphor? Take some different perspectives from other medical traditions. We are not advocating hopping from therapy to therapy, just for the sake of it. However, it is possible to be blinkered by the prevailing medical model and deny yourself the choice of treatments that may be as good or better than the one offered by orthodox medicine. There is more to medical choice than being able to choose your GP, the hospital you attend or the brand of drug you are offered.

Joseph hurt his knee some years ago and suddenly appreciated for the first time what he had taken for granted – the ability to stand up and walk without pain. He wanted to heal as quickly as possible. He saw his GP who was not sure of the problem, so referred him for an X-ray and arranged an appointment with a physiotherapist. The physiotherapist showed him some exercises he could do so he was not dependent on formal appointments. He read books about how the knee was constructed and was amazed at how beautifully it was designed to give a full range of movement. He became an expert on knees for a short time and probably bored his friends with descriptions of how they worked (or in his case did not). He took some lessons in Alexander technique and discovered how his habitual way of walking had contributed to the weakness in his knee. He saw a Feldenkreis practitioner who gave him some useful exercises and again made him aware that this was not just a 'knee' problem, it was the way he habitually moved his whole body. The knee was the weak point that gave way. He did some healing visualization exercises, used the Feldenkreis and Alexander insights to change some of the habitual ways he walked, and used weight training to strengthen particular muscles round the knee. It healed stronger than it was before. The problem was an opportunity to correct an imbalance that would have caused more problems if it had persisted.

PERCEPTUAL POSITIONS

Taking a second opinion is one aspect of an important principle in NLP – taking different perspectives. The more they differ, the more valuable the result. We learn mainly by appreciating differences. Being able to take multiple perspectives is part of the flexibility of response of successful people. The world is always richer than any one view of it and reality, it is said, leaves a lot to the imagination.

There are three main points of view in NLP:

First position is your own reality. As you are now intensely aware of your own thoughts and feelings, so you are in first position. Illness tends to put us strongly into one kind of first position.

Second position is adopting another person's point of view. You imagine what it is like for them. This is part of pacing another person, appreciating what their world is like from the inside, not judging it from the outside. Doctors who second position their patients are popular and much appreciated.

Third position is taking an outside, detached point of view. You are as objective as possible. From that position you can appreciate your relationship with others, rather than be caught up in your own view (first position) or identifying with the other person (second position).

Having these three views in a situation is called a 'triple description'. All three positions are important and the best communicators move easily between each. Health professionals need all three. They need to be clear and congruent about what they are going to do, but also to appreciate how the other person feels to help them reach a decision. They also need to be able to evaluate their work objectively. Medical science often pays too much attention to third position and misses the feelings of the real people and the patients they work with.

FOOD FOR THOUGHT

Metaphor is halfway between the unintelligible and the commonplace.

Aristotle

The highest form of generalship is to balk the enemy's plans, the next best is to prevent the junction of the enemy forces, the next in order is to attack the enemy army in the field, and the worst policy of all is to besiege walled cities.

Sun Tzu, *The Art of War*

In all fighting the direct method may be used for joining battle, but indirect methods will be needed to secure victory.

In battle there are not more than two methods of attack – the direct and the indirect – yet these two in combination give rise to an endless series of manoeuvres.

Sun Tzu, *The Art of War*

The biggest problem in the world could have been solved when it was small.

Lao Tse

Louis Pasteur's theory of germs is ridiculous fiction.

Pierre Pachet, Professor of Physiology at Toulouse, 1872

8

STRESS

From metaphor to stress. But have we moved very far? Stress is itself a metaphor. It comes from the fields of physics and engineering and describes both the force applied to a material and the resulting damage or deformation. 'Tension', 'strain' or 'feeling under pressure' are all metaphors from the same stable. We use them as if they apply to human experience in the same way as they apply to inert matter. Mechanical devices and materials can take so much stress and then they break. They have built in limitations. We have a choice. Two pieces of iron will take the same amount of stress before breaking, but people vary enormously both in what they regard as pressure and in the pressure they can handle.

Stress is also a nominalization – a noun that hides a process. Who is being stressed, by what and how?

The concept of stress was coined by Hans Selye in the 1930s.[1] He defined biological stress as the non-specific response of the body to any demand made on it. He also said stress is 'that which accelerates the rate of ageing through the wear and tear of daily living'.[2] These are useful definitions. For us, stress is the damage to your body in response to your experience. This damage comes from your body's response to events, not the event itself. The event that triggers the stress is called the 'stressor'.

It is difficult to say what stressors are, because they are different for everyone. What stresses one person is a welcome challenge to another. What events and experiences will definitely cause stress? Those that exceed your capacity to cope, or, if we stay with the

---

1 Selye, H., 'The general adaptations syndrome and the diseases of adaptation', *Journal of Clinical Endocrinology* 6 (2) (1946) 117–230
2 Selye, H., *The Stress of Life*, McGraw-Hill, 1976

metaphor of physics, those that stretch you further than your natural flexibility. Remember, flexibility is one of the four pillars of NLP. The more flexible you are, the more you can respond appropriately and stay in control, and so the less stress you experience, regardless of the demands made on you. NLP has a great deal to contribute to stress management. It shifts the focus from the outside stressor to your response and gives practical ways of building your capacity to cope.

YOUR BODY'S REACTION TO STRESS

When you meet a challenging situation, three things happen in quick succession:

* the event itself
* your perception of it
* your body's reaction to your perception of it

The event itself is unlikely to be within your control. How you perceive it is where you have control. When you experience the event as beyond your ability to cope, then the body reacts automatically, preparing to fight or flee and this stress reaction does the damage.

The reaction starts when the sympathetic part of the autonomic nervous system is activated through the hypothalamus, a small part of the brain closely connected to the limbic system which controls our emotions. The hypothalamus also regulates the body's unconscious processes, including temperature, pulse rate, breathing, water balance and blood pressure. It secretes a hormone called corticotrophin-releasing factor (CRF) which activates the pituitary gland. The pituitary secretes adrenocorticotrophin (ACTH), which triggers the adrenal gland to secrete cortisol and other hormones such as adrenaline and noradrenaline. The hormones and neuropeptides suppress the immune system. The hypothalamus also triggers the release of beta endorphins, the body's own painkillers, to enable us to withstand pain, tension and physical discomfort. The effect is to make us more alert. The pupils of our eyes dilate to let in more light and our body hair stands erect so we are more sensitive to touch and vibration. Blood flows to our large muscles and away from the digestive system. We get the same

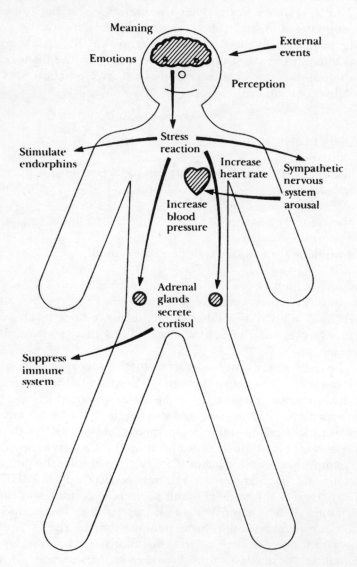

Stress reaction

biochemical jolt whether there is a real threat or not. If we think it is real, then for our bodies it *is* real.

If we are really in danger, the reaction is a very useful one. We feel alert and alive, and can go beyond our normal limits. But for some people this state of arousal becomes normal. They become addicted to stress, needing a greater and greater level to maintain the same high. Stress acts like a drug and normal life is dull by comparison. But stress increases our blood pressure, raises the heart rate, disturbs digestion and suppresses the immune system. It also impairs our thinking because blood is flowing towards the muscles and away from the rational centres of the brain. Clearly chronic stress is not good for you. It is like driving a car with the foot hard down on the accelerator whatever the traffic conditions.

The body needs time to recover after the stress reaction, to replenish the supply of hormones and neurotransmitters. Otherwise there is a roller coaster of highs and lows. This can lead to eventual 'burn out'. In the meantime, the consequences can be serious. There are better ways to feel alive and in touch with yourself and the world than relying on the biochemical cocktail of stress.

WHO GETS SICK?

Psychologists Suzanne Kobasa and Salvatore Maddi carried out a study of 200 executives at Illinois Bell Telephone Company in the mid 1970s.[3] It was a difficult time for those managers because the company was involved in some complex business deals with AT&T. All the managers filled in a questionnaire on initial stress, and a checklist of illnesses and symptoms. All were male, middle aged, middle class and married.

Although all suffered the same amount of stress only 100 reported a great deal of illness. The rest had few signs of diagnosable sickness. Kobasa found that the executives who stayed healthy had a different way of thinking about events. They considered change to be an inevitable part of life and an opportunity to grow, not a

3 Kobasa, S., 'Stressful life events, personality and health: an enquiry into hardiness', *Journal of Personality and Social Psychology* 37 (1) (1979), 1–11

threat to what they had achieved. They believed that while they could not always control what happened, they could control the impact of the problems. They were also deeply involved in their work and families, which gave them a sense of direction and excitement. Kobasa called this combination of control, commitment and willingness to accept challenge 'psychological hardiness'.

After these studies the Chicago Stress Project tracked the illnesses of 259 executives over eight years. During periods of increased work-related stress, those who were low in psychological hardiness had poorer health.[4]

CHOICE, CONGRUENCE AND CHALLENGE

We cannot avoid challenging events, so how can we cope with them?

First separate coping with the challenge from coping with the effects of stress. Some people think they are coping well when actually they are just getting used to stress. Managing existing stress is not the same as dealing with the causes.

Denial is one way of managing stress in the short term. ('Tense – who me?' said with a fixed grin, through gritted teeth.) Workaholism is another. This is an addiction and preoccupation with work rather than actual results, and allows the workaholic to ignore or justify the body's protests. Other short-term solutions are caffeine, cigarettes, alcohol, tranquillizers and many other prescription and non-prescription drugs. These can cause problems of their own.

The best way to manage stress is to avoid it. To do this you need resources to cope with potentially stressful everyday experiences.

These resources are 'the three Cs':

Choice
Congruence
Challenge

What do the three Cs mean from an NLP point of view?

4   Maddi, S., and Kobasa, S., *The Hardy Executive: Health under stress*, Dow Jones-Irwin, 1984

Choice is the ability and willingness to respond in different ways. It is flexibility in action. When you have choice, you feel in control. Another way of thinking about choice and control is when there is a balance between your perceived resources and the perceived difficulty of the challenge. If perceived difficulty is much greater than perceived resources, there is stress, panic, anxiety or confusion. However, when perceived resources are very much greater than perceived difficulty then there is boredom and carelessness. The best balance is in the middle where there is a match between perceived resources and perceived difficulty.

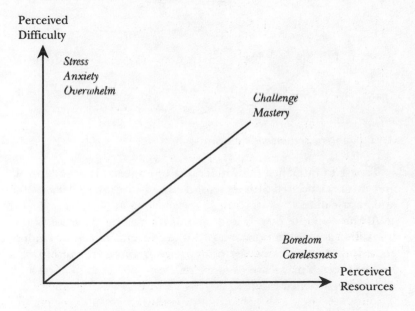

Choice comes from your control over your internal world, not the external world, which is neither predictable nor controllable.

Research shows that those people who have a high need to impress and control the external world suffer continual 'power stress'.[5] They experience double stress – they want to control

5 McClelland, D., Floor, E., Davidson, R., and Saron, C., 'Stressed power motivation, sympathetic activation, immune function and illness', *Journal of Human Stress* 6 (2) (1980), 11–19

what happens, but cannot, and so cope poorly with what does happen.

We all have an area of concern, where we care about what happens, and we all have an area of influence, where we can actually influence what happens. They overlap, but are not the same. We will not be able to influence everything that concerns us.

Area of concern and area of influence

Trying to influence the whole area of concern is over-control, and this is associated with increased risk of cardiovascular disease and gastric illness.[6]

At the opposite pole is under-control – failing to act on situations that are within our area of influence and concern. Under-control brings increased risk of depression and a feeling of helplessness, which may leave us more prone to illness in general and cancer in particular.[7]

6 Marx, J., 'Coronary artery spasms and heart disease', *Science* 208 (1980), 1127–30
7 Levy, S., 'Behaviour as a biological response modifier: the psychoneuroendocrine network and tumour immunology', *Behavioural Medicine Abstracts* 6 (1) (1985), 1–4

Look at the table below.

	Situation perceived to be within control	Situation perceived to be outside control
Action	A Effectiveness Self-efficacy Mastery	C Over-control, worry Anxiety, panic
Inaction	B Hopeless and helpless Depression	D Acceptance Ability to let go

This is a really useful way of thinking.

There is no stress in areas A and D.

Whenever you feel stress, think where you are in this diagram. Are you in box C, worrying about something that you cannot influence?

Deal with box C by letting go.

Are you in box B, feeling helpless in the face of many demands?

Deal with box B by taking action. Prioritize and deal with the important issues first. Doing nothing makes the situation worse.

Box C and box D are both unresourceful states and you need to change state before you can deal with any real problems that you might be facing. Remember you cannot adequately deal with a problem in the unresourceful state that the problem has induced.

Act in situations where you can make a difference, stay calm where you cannot – and distinguish between the two.

The second C is *congruence*. In stress-management studies it is sometimes termed 'commitment'. It is a sense of direction and energy within, that enables you to move towards what you want. It comes from having all the different parts of you working together towards what you want.

The opposite would be incongruence: a state of inner division and half-heartedness. Incongruence produces under-performance in work and in health. When you are incongruent there is no energy and no focus. Internal conflict can produce a debilitated state and this may have an effect on the immune system through the mind–body links mediated through the neurotransmitters. There is a whole continuum of incongruence. At one end there is simply feeling uncomfortable in a situation, 'pulled both ways'. This could be incongruence because you are in an unfamiliar environment and you are not sure what to do. We all experience this type of incongruence. At the other end of the continuum there is a sense of conflict about who you are – incongruence at an identity level. Conflict at this level could well be mirrored in your physiological sense of self – your immune system.

The third C is *challenge*. A sense of challenge comes from thinking in outcomes, so events are opportunities to move towards what you want. Events do not have a fixed meaning, they can mean whatever you want them to mean – you can 'reframe' them. When something happens that might cause you stress, ask:

What could this mean?
What would I like this to mean?
How could this be a useful challenge?

YOUR DEFINITION OF STRESS

Only you can define stress for yourself, which is why we have not put any stress questionnaires in this book, entertaining though they are.

How does stress affect you? We all have a weakness. Some people suffer from increased blood pressure. Headache, backache and tension in the shoulders and neck are some other signs. Indigestion, wind, decrease in the quality and quantity of your sleep for no good reason, tiredness during the day, rashes, ulcers or frequent colds and 'flu are also signs that you may be under stress. Being irritable, restless or having trouble concentrating may also be signs.

Make a list of how your body tells you about stress. This is valuable feedback.

You have to start from where you are, so pace yourself. You will not eliminate all the stress from your life overnight. Consider these questions:

How much stress is there now in my life?
Where does it come from?
Do I see any patterns?
**Do I suffer stress symptoms more at certain times – weekends,
on holiday, during work deadlines?**

There are likely to be many causes of stress. Once you know those
things that stress you that are within your field of influence, you
can start to address them. One of the best ways to analyse them is
by logical levels.

THE LOGICAL LEVELS OF STRESS

Environment

What causes you stress in the environment? There are endless
possibilities: a long journey to work, a cramped, noisy office,
household appliances that do not work, a blazing row with someone close to you. Your work could cause stress if there are many
demands upon you and you have few powers of decision. To
relieve stress, you may have to change your environment.

What resources does the environment offer to deal with
stress? One cause of stress is not knowing what will happen.
Information gives a sense of control. Studies of hospital patients
who have been given information and support about their condition have found they have a shorter stay in hospital and a speed-
ier recovery.[8]

Behaviour

What do you do that causes you stress? Examples are leaving for
appointments at the last minute, so there is constant pressure, and
meeting other people's requirements when you prefer not to.
Changes in routine may cause stress. There are many possibilities.
You will know what causes stress for yourself if you pay attention to
the feedback from your body.

8 Mumford, E., Schlesinger, H., and Glass, G., 'The effects of psychological
  intervention on recovery from surgery and heart attacks: an analysis of the
  literature', *American Journal of Public Health* 72 (2) (1982), 141–51

What behaviour do you have as a resource? Allowing more time for journeys is one example. Saying 'no' occasionally can be a great pleasure if you are used to saying 'yes' and regretting it. Alternatively, saying 'yes' if you usually say 'no' and then feel mean. Sensual pleasure is a great resource – for example, listening to music, taking the time to enjoy a good meal, spending time with children, watching a film or exercising.

Capability

If you have the ability to trigger anxiety in yourself, then you have developed a certain skill. You almost certainly will have perfected the art of imagining how something will come to an unsatisfactory conclusion. You probably do this by creating mental movies of how things could go wrong and then seeing the dire consequences. This is a skill. It demonstrates your ability to imagine so vividly that you substantially alter your body chemistry. Perhaps there are other uses for this talent. What would happen if you used the same ability to imagine vividly what it would be like 15 minutes after a *satisfactory* conclusion to the event – and then how you might have got there?

Beliefs and Values

You may not be used to thinking of beliefs and values as capable of causing stress or as resources against it, but this is the area where change can have the greatest effect. We carry our beliefs with us, so they will cause stress wherever we are. The more rigid our beliefs and expectations, the more stress we will experience, as the world is not going to go out of its way to meet our needs.

What beliefs might be stressful? A belief that people are untrustworthy and out to cheat you at every opportunity will keep you alert – and cause stress. The medical model itself is a set of stressful beliefs. It implies that when you are ill, your body is out of your control and you need to go to experts to be cured. On the other hand, a belief that you are totally responsible for healing yourself and no one can or will help you is also stressful.

All beliefs that put you at the mercy of others or events, or mean you lack choices in responding to events will contribute to stress. Values are important here, too. When you find some repetitive stress in your life, there is probably something you value at the bottom of it. What are you trying to achieve? There may be better ways to get what you want without the stress.

All beliefs that increase your sense of control, over both yourself and the external environment, are resources. A belief in your own ability to control events in your life will automatically reduce the stress you suffer. This belief is known as 'self-efficacy' and has been studied extensively by Albert Bandura and his colleagues at Stanford University.[9] They found that the more people believe they can cope with challenge, the less stress takes a toll of their bodies. People with this belief have stronger immune systems.[10]
How do you build self-efficacy?

* *By building a set of reference experiences from your own history of success and failure.*
  Notice your successes, however small. They will soon mount up. Successes only count if you were directly responsible. Instances where you got credit without putting in the work do not count.

* *By modelling others.*
  Watch others meeting the same sorts of challenges. What qualities do they use to succeed? What are the differences between those who succeed and those who fail? What do they do? What do they believe? What is important to them? If it is possible for them, why not you?

* *By finding a mentor, someone who will directly help and encourage you.*
  A mentor does not have to be a real person, they can be a character from a book or film. They do not have to be physically present, nor do you need to know them. They may be historical characters that have inspired you. When you need encouragement and help, think to yourself, 'What would they advise me to do?'

9 Bandura, A., 'Self-efficacy towards a unifying theory of behavioural change', *Psychological Review* 84 (1977), 191–215
10 Bandura, A., 'Perceived self-efficacy in the exercise of control over AIDS infection', paper presented at the National Institutes of Mental Health and Drug Abuse Research Conference on Women and AIDS, Bethseda, MD, 1987

Identity

If the stress is so great you do not know what to believe, you still have a resource – your identity. When you reach this level, you know who you are and from that, you know what to do. A strong sense of self is a great resource against stress. The only stress at this level could be a false persona. This may show in two ways. The first is interpersonal, where a person never lets anyone see their real self and is likely to work at jobs that do not allow them to express themselves. The second way a false persona may show is as a mask put on for the benefit of the self and others, to protect the real person. It may have started in childhood when the person did not know how to cope and used the persona as a means of doing so. When this happens the person will have the odd experience of feeling hollow and their behaviour will lack depth. Depth is balance in another dimension.

Beyond Identity

Finally, going beyond the limits of your present identity while incorporating it into a fuller sense of self is the greatest resource of all – and will produce a new sense of connection to others. There are many ways to achieve it, including love, religious experience and meditation. In this realm, there are no simple answers, but a possible journey, at least for a time, beyond stress.

Logical levels

	Stresses	Resources
Environment		
Behaviour		
Capability		
Beliefs and Values		
Identity		
Beyond Identity		

STRATEGY FOR DEALING WITH STRESS

When your body tells you are under stress:

1 Acknowledge the feelings in your body. Pace yourself. The feelings are real, even if you think they should not be there.

2 Focus on the stressful incident.

3 What meaning do you make of this experience?
   When you have an answer, and it will normally come quickly, ask yourself, 'What else could it mean?' And then: 'What would I like it to mean?'

4 Can you do anything about it?
   Is it within your area of influence?
   If not, let the incident go and move on.
   If it is, what resources do you have to deal with it?
   What do you want to happen in this situation?
   What is your goal?

5 What can you learn from this event, so that next time you can avoid it?

REALITY IS WHAT YOU MAKE IT

NLP, in common with many other systems of psychology and philosophy, suggests we do not see the world as it really is, but construct a model of it. Our perceptions are filtered through our senses, and we interpret our experiences in the light of our beliefs, interests, upbringing, preoccupations and state of mind. We draw a map and navigate through life with it. If it is a good map we will go far and enjoy the journey. A limited map guarantees a limited journey. We all travel through the same territory, but with different maps. Throughout history, people have fought and died in arguments over whose map is right. NLP is not about giving you the 'right' map, but it does purport to show you something of map-making. It can also broaden the map you have, so you can experience a more interesting journey.

NLP suggests we create our maps in three main ways:

- First, we delete parts of our experience. Of all the possible sights, sounds, feelings, tastes and smells that are available to us, we are aware of only a few. Deletion is essential – we would be overwhelmed if we were not selective about where to put our attention. We filter our experience on the basis of our beliefs, interests and state of health. If you have ever ignored a pain in order to get a job done or searched for keys that were under your nose, you know what deletion is.
- Secondly we distort, by giving weight to some parts of our experience and diminishing other parts. Distortion is how we create meaning and value from what happens to us. Without it we have only a dull, grey world of facts and figures. Distortion is the basis of creativity and art. It is also the basis of suspicion, paranoia and misunderstanding. It is how we make meaning of our symptoms. For example, a person may blame another for giving them a cold, despite the fact that they have been in contact with people with colds thousands of times without catching one themselves.
- Thirdly, we generalize from experiences by deducing rules from a small number of instances. We learn by generalizing.

For example, we learn to do any calculation by learning the laws of arithmetic from a small number of problems. Beliefs are generalizations. Generalizing is essential: we meet the unknown based on what we know. It is only a problem if we pick the wrong example to generalize from or do not stay open to new experience. For example, if one person has cheated us, it would be foolish to generalize and assume that everybody is dishonest.

We all delete, distort and generalize. But, just as with representational systems, people tend towards one of the three, so some people do more deleting, others more distorting and still others more generalizing. The three processes themselves are useful, it is how we apply them that can lead to trouble.

People who delete a great deal may not be sensitive to their bodies. Deleting pain and discomfort, they may push themselves too far and ignore the warnings their bodies give them. They may also delete information about how others feel and may appear insensitive. People who distort may be hypersensitive to their own feelings, perhaps to the point of hypochondria. They may be very sensitive to others, reading meaning into what others say and do. People who generalize too much may be rather inflexible and follow set rules of conduct, expecting others to do the same. They may try to apply yesterday's solution to a current problem and find it hard to cope with change.

GENERALIZATION CAN DAMAGE YOUR HEALTH

Certain ways of thinking increase the risk of illness. Dr Martin Seligman and his colleagues at the University of Pennsylvania have carried out studies into what they call 'attributional style' – how we explain what happens to us.[11]

The first way is the pessimistic style. This is not about looking for misfortune, but a way of explaining it when it befalls. It has three components:

11 Seligman, M., 'Helplessness and explanatory style: risk factors for depression and disease', paper presented at the annual meeting of the Society of Behavioural Medicine, San Francisco, March 1986
   also Peterson, C., and Seligman, M., 'Causal explanations as a risk factor for depression: theory and evidence', *Psychological Review* 91 (3) (1984), 347–74

- People who use this style assume any misfortune is their fault. They blame themselves, deleting external factors and generalizing by taking all of the responsibility. For this to make sense they also simplify the event and this is a form of distortion.
- They tend to think the situation will persist. Nothing is going to change, the world is stable. They generalize from one event to thinking life will always be that way.
- Thirdly, they generalize again and think it will affect everything they do.

This triple pessimistic pattern of thinking is known as ISG (internal, stable, global) in medical literature. It leads to what Seligman calls 'learned helplessness' – giving up because it seems as if nothing will make a difference. This is a lethal pattern, leading to depression and a feeling of general helplessness, and brings an increased risk of illness.

DEPRESSION STRATEGY – CATASTROPHIZING

The following strategy is known as 'catastrophizing':

- Blame yourself. It's all your fault. The outside world is fine. What is more, tell yourself it is because of the sort of person you are (identity), not what you did (behaviour).

- Think that things will always be this way, nothing will change. Nothing you can do will make a difference.

- Expect it to affect everything you do.

When anything goes well, reverse this procedure:

- Tell yourself it's just a lucky break and nothing to do with you or let other people take all the credit.

- Tell yourself it will not last.

- Expect it to have little or no effect on the rest of your life.

The other attributional style is optimism. This is external, unstable, specific (EUS). External causes are given due weight, there is no self-blame. Events are seen in context, not generalized.

Neither optimism or pessimism can be true, both are impossible to prove. They are different ways of looking at the world. Given the choice, choose the healthier way – optimism.

OPTIMISM STRATEGY

Use deletion, distortion and particularly generalization to make you healthier. Think about unpleasant experiences as:

- A combination of outside circumstances allied to your reaction. It is not failure, but feedback for you about your behaviour, not the person you are.

- An isolated incident. Think about what you could have done differently to avoid the suffering, so that you can learn from the experience.

- A specific incident that will have little effect, if any, on your other activities.

When something goes well, reverse this way of thinking:

- Take some personal credit.

- Remember all the other occasions when events went well. This one adds to the pattern.

- Think of ways that it will affect your life and how you can learn from it so you have similar good fortune in the future.

OPTIMISM AND HEALTH –
THE HARVARD STUDY

There have been a number of studies that relate an optimistic style of thinking to health. One study was done over 35 years, in conjunction with the Harvard Study of Adult Development, using a group of healthy and successful members of the Harvard classes from 1942 to 1944.[12] The subjects' habitual level of optimism or pessimism was initially elicited through a questionnaire. Every five years the subjects had a thorough medical examination. As they aged, their health tended to worsen. However, although all started extremely healthy, the gap between the most healthy and least healthy became larger as time went by. Of the 99 men studied, 13 died before the age of 60. The results were simple and unequivocal. Overall, men who used optimistic explanations for bad events at age 25 were healthier later in life (after the age of 40), than men who offered pessimistic explanations. The benefits were particularly noticeable between the ages of 40 and 45. The health of the pessimistic group showed a marked deterioration that could not be accounted for by any other variable.

The results were statistically significant: there was less than 1 chance in 1,000 that they were random. The link between cigarette smoking and the development of lung cancer is less statistically robust.

RELATIONSHIP AND RAPPORT

Relationships are a primary source of stress in most people's lives. A number of good quality relationships are probably the best way you can support your health and well-being. A good relationship with yourself is the place to start. Every kind of misunderstanding and conflict we encounter from the outside can also occur within

12 Peterson, C., Seligman, M., and Valliant, G., 'Pessimistic explanatory style is a risk factor for physical illness: a thirty five year longitudinal study', *Journal of Personality and Social Psychology* 55 (1988), 23–7
see also Peterson, C., and Bossio, L., *Health and Optimism*, The Free Press, 1991, pp.25–31 for a summary of this experiment

us. How well the different parts of us live together is a mirror of how we relate to others.

Rapport – that quality of trust and responsiveness – is the basis of good relationships. Rapport is built by pacing at every logical level. Rapport with yourself is built by pacing yourself. Acknowledge your feelings, pay attention to your body and your inner environment. Give your body the rest, exercise and nutrition it needs. Acknowledge what you do and what you are capable of doing, without initially trying to change it. Acknowledge your beliefs and values, being true to what you choose to believe and what is important to you. Acknowledge your identity, the person you are, not as a fixed icon, but as a changing and evolving being. This will open the way to going beyond identity.

To create rapport with others, pace *them* at every logical level. Affirm their identity, treat them for who they are, not who you think they ought to be. It is so easy to create ogres or icons of others and then respond to the masks, not the people. Then pace their beliefs and values. You do not have to agree with them, just acknowledge them. Thirdly, pace their capabilities, Respect their ways of thinking and acting. Acknowledge their skills. You can pace their behaviour, using body matching and voice matching for the purposes of rapport. This an area which NLP has studied in depth and is described in full in other NLP publications.[13]

A MIRROR ON RELATIONSHIP

We would like to give you a process to explore any type of relationship, particularly a stressful one. Relationship is two-way traffic and sometimes we are so concerned about changing the other person that we do not notice that what we are doing is part of the problem. Being able to change your responses is within your control. But you will need to see things afresh.

First, think of the person you have difficulty with.

Imagine you are back with them. Associate into that memory. How would you label their behaviour? 'Hostile', 'passive', 'withdrawing'? What feelings do you have towards the other person?

---

13 *See* O'Connor, J., and McDermott, I., *Principles of NLP*, Thorsons, 1996
 also O'Connor, J., and Seymour, J., *Introducing NLP*, Thorsons, 1990

For example, you may feel angry, frustrated or helpless. These are your own feelings about them in that situation. This is your first position response to the other person in that relationship.

On what logical level do you think the conflict takes place? Is it about behaviour, does it challenge your beliefs or does it threaten your identity?

Then break state, think of something different.

Secondly, take second position. Imagine you are the other person. As that other person, what is the experience like for you?

What are you trying to accomplish? What do you feel about the relationship?

Break state and come back to yourself.

Now, go outside the relationship and become a detached observer. This is going to third position. A good way to do this is to imagine a stage in front of you. See both of you on stage. See that other person doing what they do. See yourself responding to them.

Shift your question from 'How can I change that person's behaviour?' to 'How am I reinforcing or triggering that person's behaviour?'

How else could you respond to that person? What prompts you to continue doing what you do in this relationship?

What could you do differently that would mean it would be impossible for them to respond in the old way? What emotional state would be a resource for you in that situation?

Perhaps they too are seeking a new way but do not know how to break out of the old pattern. It is very rare that a relationship is uncomfortable for only one of the people.

What do you feel about your actions in that situation?

What advice would you give yourself in that situation?

Are you exasperated at your inability to influence the other person?

Is this exasperation useful?

All these questions help to get a new perspective, especially as our relationship with ourselves so often reflects our relationship to others.

Finally, keep in mind what you want in that relationship.

Do you want it to continue in its present form?

What are the advantages of it as it is?
What sort of positive relationship do you want?
What can you do to achieve it?

FOOD FOR THOUGHT

An optimist may see a light where there is none, but why must the pessimist always run to blow it out?

Michel de Saint-Pierre

God, give us the grace to accept with serenity the things that cannot be changed, courage to change the things that should be changed, and the wisdom to distinguish one from the other.

Reinhold Niebuhr

The music that can deepest reach and cure all ill is cordial speech.

Emerson

The man who is a pessimist before the age of forty eight knows too much: if he is an optimist after that, he knows too little.

Mark Twain

The optimist proclaims that we live in the best of all possible worlds, and the pessimist fears that this is true.

James Cabell

A pessimist is someone who, when confronted with two unpleasant choices, selects both.

Anon

Change and pain are part of life, but suffering is optional.

Anon

WORRY AND HOPE

> In the absence of certainty, there is nothing wrong with hope.
> Carl Simonton

Worry is stressful and fully deserves a section to itself. It is bad enough when disaster strikes, but worry about the consequences compounds it. Worse still, we often worry about what may happen, but has not. We feel bad in advance for no reason. The situation may be imaginary, but the stress it creates is real enough. Worry can banish sleep, and lead to low back pain and gastro-intestinal problems such as wind and colitis. And even when the problems are real, worry does nothing to resolve them.

We are capable of worrying over *anything*. There are innumerable ways events can go wrong. The more you have, the more you have to worry over. We worry about ourselves, our loved ones, especially our children. If that is not enough, there are work-related worries and global worries: overpopulation, global warming and the break up of the ozone layer. Worry is concern about bad future scenarios. Its opposite is hope – looking for a good or better future.

Like all states of mind, worry has a structure that NLP can study. Once you know the structure you can change it.

THE STRUCTURE OF WORRY

Worry has some typical features:

- There is a lot of thinking, but no action. Worry inhibits action.
- Worry sets you up as either completely responsible or

completely helpless. Cause and effect are like two opposite
ends of a seesaw. One type of worry drops you all alone at the
causal end. You may think that you are completely accountable
for what will happen, that everything hinges on your actions
and when it goes wrong, you will be blamed. The other type of
worry is equally uncomfortable. Now you are on the effect side
of the seesaw, at the mercy of events that land on the other
end and hurl you metaphorically aloft. You may think that you
are totally at the mercy of events. These are simplifications.
The real world is much more complicated. We can influence
events, but do not have complete control over them, nor they
over us.

- Worry is not directed *towards* an outcome; it moves *away* from
  undesirable events. In order to move away, you have to create
  undesirable consequences to move away from. So you imagine
  that everything that can go wrong will go wrong – usually in
  unwelcome detail. Outcome thinking is the opposite of worry,
  because by moving towards a goal, you start making a plan of
  action and this robs worrying of its power.
- There is no check from the external world. Worry goes round
  in circles, it is like being trapped in a drawing by Escher where
  you lose perspective and find yourself at the bottom of the
  same spiral just when you hoped to emerge at the top. It is
  built one loop inside another. The loops never complete, they
  are built of imaginary events, so they cannot be resolved,
  because another possibility takes you in again. The only way to
  resolve them is to do something in the real world – get more
  information, make a telephone call, talk to other people to get
  other views.

Worry is a strategy – a sequence of thought and behaviour – and it
often runs automatically.

The sequence usually starts with an internal voice that says
something like, 'Suppose X were to happen?' Next, we make
mental pictures of the unpleasant possibilities of X. The pictures
are constructed and usually close, moving and associated, as if they
were happening now, rather than on our future timeline. Looking
at these pictures, we feel bad – just as we would if the events were
actually happening.

NLP has a shorthand way of expressing different types of
thinking:

Internal dialogue is written as A^i_d (auditory internal dialogue).

Constructed pictures are written as V^i_c (visual internal constructed).

Feelings are written as K^i (kinesthetic internal).

The structure of worry

Triggering event
↓
Internal dialogue (A^i_d):
'What if ... X ... were to happen?'
↓
Constructed, associated, moving pictures of the bad events (V^i_c)
↓
Bad feelings (K^i)
↓
More internal dialogue

BREAKING THE WORRY LOOP

Worry does not lead anywhere, so how do you stop it?

First, know your own worry strategy. It will probably be very familiar, some variation and enhancement of the basic strategy.

To get out of the loop, you first have to realize you are inside it. That means you have to jump out and dissociate from it. See it for what it is – a thought sequence that leads nowhere.

Once you are outside, see it in all its boring familiarity and break state. Be aware of your body in the present moment. How is it feeling? Notice how that awareness changes your state.

Now ask, 'What has to be true for this to be realistic? Is there any evidence that these things will happen?' Often you will find a whole set of very unlikely circumstances all have to combine. Your worrying scenario has all the probability of being struck by lightning after winning the lottery.

What is the positive intention behind worrying? What is it of value you are trying to accomplish? Preparing and planning for bad events. This is important, but worry is not the best way to do it. Worry may also be drawing your attention to a subject you have been avoiding which needs to be resolved.

Use these insights to change the original worry question. Instead of asking, 'What if X were to happen?', ask instead, 'What will I do if X happens?' This has three effects:

- It puts the events into the future.
- It dissociates you from them.
- It changes your attention from the events to your actions.

You can now plan what to do and not be stuck inside the scenario with all the bad feelings that go with it. Ask yourself, 'Is this likely to happen?' Do you need to think of a plan now or is it so unlikely that you can ignore it? Or maybe you can trust in your own competence to act for the best at the time.

If you do need to plan now, what do you want to happen? Work on an outcome. Make mental movies of what you might do and stay dissociated, outside the movies. Run through several possibilities. Select the one that gives you the best feeling. Associate into that movie and mentally rehearse it. If it feels good, you have a plan. You may want two or three choices, so mentally rehearse a few movies that satisfy you. Then break state, shift your physiology into a more resourceful state and go and do something else.

Do you know your favourite times to worry? You may have developed the habit at certain times of day, Sunday evening maybe. In bed before you go to sleep is a favourite worry time, perhaps to get your attention when your guard is down. If there is an issue to resolve, arrange to think about it the next day. Keep your promise or it will return with redoubled force the next night.

Worry breaker strategy

1 Internal dialogue (A^i_d): 'What will I do if ... X ... happens'?
↓
2 Make constructed, dissociated, moving pictures (V^i_c) of a number of possibilities.
↓
3 Choose one that makes you feel good (K^i).
↓
4 Mentally rehearse that plan, taking the action and getting the result you want by running a visual, constructed, associated, moving picture (V^i_c).

↓

5 Notice this makes you feel good (K^i). Go back to step 2 if you want more choices.

↓

6 Break state.

Suppose you go through this sequence and it seems there is nothing you can do? Then there is nothing you can do. Accept the situation as it is for the moment. It may change. Nothing is predictable. You may need more information. If so, think about how you will get it. The most extreme question would be: 'What will happen if I die?' If this is a real possibility, then one choice is to prepare for as good a death as possible. We will look at death in Chapter 12.

TALKING OURSELVES DOWN

Worry usually begins with internal dialogue. A lot of internal dialogue is of little use and some is stressful. Sometimes we would not dream of speaking to anyone else the way we speak to ourselves. Any limiting beliefs and presuppositions we have will turn up in internal dialogue.

When we talk to ourselves we use words just as we do when we talk to others. However, sometimes we forget that language is a way of representing experience, not the experience itself. One of the first NLP models developed by Richard Bandler and John Grinder in 1975 is known as the Meta Model, a series of key questions to unravel the possible misleading effects of language.[1] These questions are excellent for clarifying communication between people. Here we will use some of them to explore what you say to yourself.

We know that our thoughts have real effects on our nervous system. We suggest your immune system is eavesdropping on your internal dialogue. Perhaps it is even obeying the suggestions without you knowing. Therefore cleaning up your internal dialogue could have a very beneficial effect on your internal state and on the robustness of your immune system.

---

1 Bandler, R., and Grinder, J., *The Structure of Magic 1*, Science and Behaviour Books, 1975

The first step is to become aware of your internal dialogue. Most people have an internal voice; for some it is loud and insistent, for others it is barely audible. Have you ever noticed which direction it comes from? What sort of voice tone does it use? Is it a pleasure to listen to? Whose voice is it? Your own? If it belongs to someone else, did you give them permission to come into your mind? A nagging, blaming voice tone from the outside is stressful – and so is one from the inside.

Does your internal voice make any comparisons? Comparisons are shown by words like 'better', 'best', 'worse', 'worst', 'more', 'less'. Discover if you have any demotivating, unrealistic comparisons in your mind. When you hear yourself making a comparison of how you did (behaviour) or the sort of person you are (identity), make sure you know the basis of the comparison. For example, 'I did badly.' The best question to ask is, 'Compared with what?' Your best? Your ideal? An expert? Unrealistic comparisons are depressing, but first you have to know they are unrealistic. To motivate yourself, compare where you are with an inspiring future, not with other people. To judge your progress, compare where you are with where you started.

We have already seen how we can create stress by generalizing. One way you will know you are generalizing is when you hear words like 'all', 'never', 'always' and 'every'. These words are known as 'universals'. They imply there are no exceptions. Examples are, 'I could never do that', 'I always get a cold at Christmas', 'Everyone is going to laugh at me.' Set down in cold print the flaw in the reasoning is obvious. Nothing could be so absolute, there are surely exceptions. Remember what they are. If you truly cannot find an exception, are you happy with that state of affairs? If not, resolve to create an exception at the first opportunity.

Your inner voice may also be setting rules and making judgements. We often make judgements that are not based on good evidence. Doctors have an air of authority, and they know a good deal about disease and illness in the abstract, but you are the expert of your subjective experience. When you find yourself telling yourself what you should or should not do, start asking, 'Why?' or 'Who says?'

We set rules for ourselves with words like 'should' and 'shouldn't', 'must' and 'ought', 'can' and 'can't'. These words are called 'modal operators' in linguistics. Be particularly watchful for these in your internal dialogue. We grow up bombarded with modal operators from parents and teachers. They are one of the principal ways we set boundaries. However, these boundaries may be out of date or unreasonably limiting. When you hear yourself saying you 'should', 'must' or 'ought to' do something, stop and ask, 'What would happen if I did not?' There may be a good reason, but there may not. Explore the consequences. You need not blindly obey. Another choice is to replace every 'should' you uncover in your internal dialogue with 'can'. So 'I must get well' becomes 'I can get well.' 'I can' is empowering – you can do it, do you want to?

Take a similar approach to 'shouldn't' and 'mustn't'. Ask yourself, 'What would happen if I did?' and explore the consequences. Whenever you hear yourself saying 'can't' in your internal dialogue, immediately ask, 'What stops me?' There may be a good reason, but it may be a limiting belief. Once you turn it round by asking that question, it sets you on the path to discovering blocks that you can overcome. These modal operators often hide beliefs and assumptions about health and illness. After you have queried them, ask yourself what beliefs underlie them.

We have already dealt with abstract nouns (nominalizations) at length *(see pp.113–16)*. Any medical condition will be described using a nominalization. Nominalizations are frozen in time, you cannot change them. But what is happening? Turn it into a process. Find out what is actually taking place in your body. However serious an illness, the first step in gaining some control is to denominalize it.

Lastly, listen to your internal dialogue for any tendency to blame yourself. Self-blame implies you had total responsibility and caused the effect. We know that the law of cause and effect cannot apply so simplistically to human affairs, but the English language does not make this distinction. We use the same form of expression in 'He made me angry' and 'He made the glass break.' When you say something like 'She made me ill' you make yourself powerless and give someone else the power over your health. When you find yourself attributing your emotional state to external people or circumstances, ask yourself, 'How exactly is this making me...?' The deeper question is, 'How exactly am I contributing to this state or to my illness?' As long as you set the cause completely outside yourself, you are just suffering the effect and have little power over your state.

Here are some examples of how to question your internal dialogue:

'I should do more exercise.'
What would happen if I did not?

'I can't give up smoking.'
What stops me?

'I can't find time to exercise.'
What stops me?

'I should be healthier.'
Healthier compared to what or whom?

'I mustn't ask for help.'
What would happen if I did?

'He makes me feel stressed.'
How exactly does he do that?

'I have diabetes.'
What exactly is happening in my body that goes under the name of 'diabetes'?

PANDORA'S BOX

Have you heard the Greek myth of Pandora's box? Pandora, the first woman, was given a box and instructed not to open it, but not told why. For her, life was idyllic, as in the parallel myth of the Garden of Eden. However, once again the forbidden fruit was irresistible and Pandora opened the box. Out burst all the evils of the world in the form of stinging insects. They swarmed out, stung Pandora and escaped jubilantly into the world like a host of malevolent genies. One creature was left in the box – hope. Hope had to plead to be let out, for Pandora was scared to open the box a second time. When she did, hope consoled her.

The myth is rich in meaning. One thing it tells us is that there is always hope. Hope is the opposite of worry and depression; it holds the promise of a better future. 'False hope' is a contradiction. All hope is real hope if it leads you to action that sets out to bring the future you want into the present moment.

Hope is meaningless unless it inspires action. It is not an excuse to wait passively for things to improve but an inspiration to mould a worthwhile future.

KNOWING WHAT YOU WANT

People often take hope as if it were a commodity or a thing – 'You must have hope.' But hope is also a verb – something we do. When we hope, we are imagining a better future. What future do we want? How much better? A better future is something we create for ourselves, first in our minds, then in reality. The first step is the first pillar of NLP – know what you want. That means creating what you want.

The question to ask is, 'What do I want?' This generates outcomes that move you towards a desired state.

Instead, we often ask, 'What's the problem?' This focuses on what is wrong in the present state and does not move you forward. Indeed, it is liable to pull you into the past with secondary questions like 'Why do I have this problem?', 'How does it limit me?' and 'Who is to blame?'

None of these are particularly useful. They do nothing to create a better future or to build hope. If we want to change the present, then exploring the archaeology of the problem is not enough. Nor does blaming help. Blame is a unpleasant cocktail of guilt and responsibility, to drink or to offer to others. It is based once again on a simplistic idea of cause and effect.

You are creating your own future by what you do now. Thinking about what you want – your outcomes – is the key to making the future how you want it to be.

When you set outcomes for your health, or other areas of your life, there are a few useful rules to remember:

- *Express your health outcome in the positive.*
  Move towards a desired future, not away from an undesirable present. They are not the same. Moving towards a desired future will automatically take you from the limitations of the present. But just moving away from the present could take you anywhere. It could be worse. All you know is that it will be different.
  There are two very common health goals – to stop smoking and to lose weight. One of the reasons they are so difficult to

achieve is that they are both expressed in the negative. Anything that has the words 'give up', 'lose' or 'cut down ' is negative. Thinking about losing weight automatically focuses on what you have now – weight. Thinking about all the sweets and biscuits you should not eat just turns your attention to those delicious candies. No wonder it is so difficult, you are constantly focusing on what you have. Make losing weight part of a wider outcome of being healthier.

To turn a negative outcome into a positive ask: 'What would this goal do for me if I got it?' or 'What do I want instead?' For example, 'giving up smoking' may become 'having healthy lungs', 'being more healthy', 'fitter' or 'having more money'.

- *Make your health outcomes as specific as possible and be clear what is within your area of influence.*
  Give your goals a time limit – when do you want them?
  Where do you want them and with whom?
  What are you going to do in order to get them?
  A goal that relies on other people doing it all for you or the world miraculously handing you what you want on a plate, with no effort on your part, is the passive kind of hoping that achieves little.
  What is directly under your control and what will need the help of others?
  How will you persuade them to help you?

- *What resources do you have to achieve these health outcomes?*
  Resources come in different forms. There may be people who will help you, possessions, money, role models. Resources are personal qualities such as persistence and intelligence.
  Role models are resources – if you know someone who has achieved something you want to achieve, find out how they did it. If it was possible for them, why not for you?

- *How will you know you have this health outcome?*
  What exactly will you see?
  What exactly will you hear?
  What exactly will you feel?
  What will you taste and smell?
  What is the very last piece of evidence before you get the outcome?

Make sure the evidence you choose comes through your senses.

For example, evidence for being more healthy might be that you have a 32in (81cm) waist, you wake up feeling alert and breathing easily instead of coughing, you have lost 10 pounds in weight, your complexion has improved, your sense of taste has improved, you laugh at least six times a day and at least one friend tells you that you look better than before.

Trust your senses. By thinking about what you will see, hear and feel when you have achieved your outcome, you are creating images and sounds that make the future real. That makes them motivating, because for your brain, they are real.

- *When you have decided your outcome, you may need to split it into a number of smaller ones to achieve it.*
  For example, an outcome to become more healthy might best be split into outcomes about healthy eating, building an exercise plan, setting aside time to relax each day, spending more time with your loved ones and finding out more about a branch of complementary medicine that appeals to you.

- *Think about the wider consequences of achieving your outcome.*
  Health outcomes affect many aspects of your life. They may even change your identity. Possible consequences are moving house, buying new clothes, making new relationships, spending money, changing eating habits and getting up earlier in the morning. What is fine from your point of view may bring you into conflict with others. Take second position with the significant other people in your life.
  How will they be affected?
  What will they think about you achieving your goal?
  How will they act differently towards you?
  What else would happen?
  What might you have to sacrifice? Think of the time, money and effort, both mental and physical, you will need to invest. Is the goal worth it?
  What are the benefits of the present situation? There must be some or you would not be there. Make sure you keep those benefits or find another way to get them in the future that suits you better.

- *Lastly, and most important, do you feel congruent about this outcome?* Does it express the essential you? Check for incongruence and change the outcome if necessary – make it smaller or check the consequences more carefully. When you are sure it is congruent with your sense of self, make an action plan. There is software available that will take you through this whole process *(see Resources section page 219).*

CHECKLIST FOR HEALTH OUTCOMES

Is your outcome expressed in the positive, moving towards something you want, rather than away from something you do not want?
Is it specific and simple?
Does it have a time limit?
Are you clear where, when and with whom you want this outcome?

What resources do you have to achieve it?
For example, possessions, personal qualities, people and role models.

How will you know you have achieved it?
What will you see, hear and feel?

What are the wider consequences of achieving your outcome?
What will you have to give up?
How will others be affected?
What money, mental and physicaleffort will it take?
Is it worth it?
How can you incorporate the good things about the present situation into the outcome?

Is it *you?*

Act!

COMPELLING FUTURES

Now you can start to create a compelling future by placing your outcomes on your timeline. This process was created from the ideas of John Grinder, Richard Bandler and Tad James. You can use this process for putting specific goals into your future or in a more general way.

First, take some outcomes from the following areas:

- physical
- professional
- social
- emotional
- spiritual

This is *your life*. If you do not have outcomes in these areas, then start making some!

If you do not yet have any specific outcomes, then imagine how you want to be. What attributes do you want?

Imagine your timeline running from past to future. You can do this mentally, but you can also use some floor space so you can walk up and down the timeline from past to future. Whichever makes the process more real and immediate for you is good.

Mark a spot on your timeline as now.(1)

Go along your timeline as far back into your past as you have set outcomes in the future. If you are creating a compelling future five years in the future, then go back five years into your past.(2)

Look forward to the point you have marked as 'now'. You created that 'now' by all the actions you took in the past.

Go forward to 'now' and get a sense of how much you have changed in that time. Certain key experiences may come to mind.(3)

Come off your timeline (4) and make a dissociated picture of yourself achieving your outcome in the future. See yourself as you wish to be. Add any sounds and voices that belong there. Now associate into that picture.

What does it feel like?

Adjust the submodalities of the picture, making the picture bigger, brighter and more colourful until you get the best feeling. Experiment with the auditory submodalities until you are satisfied.

When you are completely satisfied, come out of the picture and disassociate.

Take the picture along your timeline into the future to where

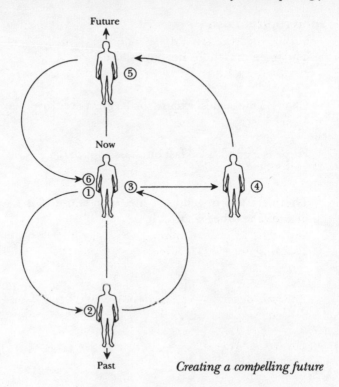

Creating a compelling future

you want to achieve that outcome. Put that dissociated picture into your timeline.(5)

Now look back from this position in the future towards the present.

What steps do you need to take to make this future a reality?

What are the likely obstacles that might stop you and how can you circumvent them?

What has to happen between now and then?

Notice the steps and stages of the process.

Come back to now.(6)

You will have realized that there are a number of specific outcomes to achieve to arrive where you want to go.

Always have goals to look forward to. When you run out, create more. If the ones you have lose their appeal, create different ones. Always have a dream beyond the dream you are living.

FOOD FOR THOUGHT

The main reason for healing is love.

Paracelsus

Chaos is the sexiest excuse for laziness ever invented.

Bruce Sterling

Hope is a good breakfast but a bad supper.

Francis Bacon

There are two tragedies in life. One is not to get your heart's desire. The other is to get it.

George Bernard Shaw

PAIN AND PLEASURE

> There is no cure for birth and death but to enjoy the interval.
> George Santayana

This chapter is about paying attention to your experience. This is the most important message in this book. Paying attention to yourself is the basis of self-esteem. It expands your sense of self. It is also central to your health.

Our bodies are giving us feedback every moment about our state. We tend to put our experience into one of three classes: pleasure we seek; pain we avoid; and everything in between we ignore or tolerate. Pain is uncomfortable feedback. In pain we are most alone, most isolated, caught in our bodies. Human sympathy makes pain more tolerable, we feel we are not alone. Paying attention to your experience of pain will change it, as a step towards relieving and dealing with it. Pleasure is sought-after feedback. Your senses are the doorways to physical pleasure. Pleasure is one experience of health. Pleasure takes us outside ourselves. Whereas in pain we may be closed off, in pleasure we open out, we share, we connect with ourselves, others and the world.

Much of our life is spent in between, skating on the surface of experience, and because we often pay little attention to what we are experiencing in the here and now, we deny ourselves the pleasure of being. Then we are driven to seek ever more distractions to pull our attention outwards. We miss what is, in favour of what might be or what has been. The present is all we have, it is the only place we can actually experience pleasure, but we give little attention to it.

PAIN

There are many forms of pain, both physical and emotional. We will concentrate on physical pain, although all we say can also apply to emotional pain.

Pain is real, yet difficult to define. It is subjective – only the person in pain can describe it, although we have a poor vocabulary to do so considering how important it is. There is no magic medical instrument that the doctor can use to find out objectively how much pain you are in, but there is no such thing as imaginary pain. Pain is always real to the sufferer. Real pain is whatever you decide it is. Children's pain in particular has been neglected. Children may be smaller than adults, but their pain is not smaller to them. It may be greater because of the fear and confusion they suffer. Pain relief is not a luxury and it is really important to believe what people say about their pain.

Some parts of our bodies are sensitive, we know exactly where the pain is. Some causes and signs of pain, like blood or broken bones, may be visible, although the pain itself is not. Injury in an area with few pain receptors will hurt somewhere else – the pain will be 'referred'. Internal organs have few pain receptors, so for example in the early stages of a heart attack, pain is felt down the left arm.

It seems likely that everyone has much the same pain threshold, but not the same pain tolerance. States such as fear, helplessness and confusion make physical pain worse. A toothache is very painful, but the cause and the remedy are known. We know the pain will have an end and that makes it more bearable. Childbirth is painful, but there is great joy too and a purpose that makes the pain bearable. Pain is worse when it has no explanation; uncertainty is hard to bear. We do not know what to do or how to stop such pain, so we feel helpless. A nagging, unexplained chest pain could be more troublesome than a toothache, because of the worry that goes with it.

Acute pain is sudden, intense and lasts a short time. It either goes away by itself or we act to make it go away. Chronic pain is harder to deal with. It causes great suffering and can destroy the quality of life, causing depression and helplessness.

PAIN AS FEEDBACK

Pain deserves attention and respect. It is a signal, feedback from your body that something is wrong and needs attention. We write here of normal, acute pains and symptoms of illness that most people experience in the course of living. Serious, chronic pain may need medical and drug treatment, although there is much that can be done to complement drug treatment. Management of chronic pain is an area of medicine that is fast developing. Methods are being introduced so patients can control their own pain-relieving medication – at last a recognition that standard doses do not suit everyone.

Although the word 'pain' comes from the Latin *poena*, the same root as 'punishment', pain is an inevitable and essential part of being alive. Without pain we would have to pay attention consciously to everything we did in case we injured ourselves and it would make life impossible. If you did not feel pain when you touched a flame you might seriously damage your hand. Pain tells us to stop what you are doing. Often the reflex does not even give you time to think about it. Pain forces us to take action. The pain of an inflamed appendix drives us to seek help or die. You would not really wish away the pain signal. Pain is healthy. It is your body telling you, 'I'm alive!' Only when pain is constant and you cannot take action to relieve it does it become a problem rather than a friend.

DRUGS

When we think of pain relief, we usually think of drugs. Even endorphins, the substances we produce naturally to relieve pain, are called the body's 'natural painkilling drugs'. There are quite a few strange presuppositions embedded in that metaphor! Endorphins work by occupying the receptor sites so the neuro-transmitters that transmit the pain message cannot be received. Cocaine works in the same way.

Advertisements for drugs commend them as 'painkillers'. (There's that metaphor again.) Medicine encourages the pain-killing approach – take a drug at the first twinge.

Drugs do have an important place in treating pain and there are dozens of them on the market that are safe and effective. So why not use them? In fact the fewer painkillers you take the better, for many reasons. First, you neglect your internal resources. Rather than assume you have no control and need to look outside yourself, explore what control you do have.

Second, the more you take them, the more habituated you will become and the less effective they will be. The less you take them, the more effective they will be when you really need them.

Third, pain is a messenger, a symptom, not a cause. We need to hear and understand what the pain is trying to tell us before we kill the messenger. When you use a pain-relieving drug, you may lose the pain, but the cause of the pain will be untouched. With the pain gone you may continue doing more of the very thing that is causing the pain, only now you will not realize it. Would you anaesthetize your hand so you could leave it longer in a flame?

To take another example, allergies and muscle tension are common causes of headaches. An aspirin will relieve the ache, but does nothing for the allergy or stressful situation that is causing the headache. This could lead to more severe headaches, until aspirin does not work any more.

Another example is continually using steroids to reduce inflammation and pain of muscle or tendon injury, especially in sports. Steroids are powerful drugs, allied to the naturally produced stress hormone cortisol. They are immune system suppressive and may have other serious side-effects. Pain tells you the muscle is damaged and needs to recover. The drug stops that signal, but the muscle is still damaged. Continuing to use it courts more serious injury. The price of playing on may be very high – back pain from damaged vertebrae or arthritis.

With emotional pain the same argument applies. Doctors tend to prescribe tranquillizers with the best of intentions. However, tranquillizers do not remove the cause or resolve the issue, but blunt the senses. They take away the ability to feel. For example, grieving is a natural process to heal the pain of loss and it needs time to complete. Tranquillizers may block the grieving process. There are many techniques in NLP for resolving phobias, dealing with guilt, loss and past trauma that are beyond the scope of this book, but are fully described in NLP literature.[1] These techniques work, not by suppressing symptoms, but by offering means to address the issues that have created those symptoms.

1 *See* O'Connor, J., and Seymour, J., *Introducing NLP*, Thorsons, 1990

Drugs have their place. It can be appropriate to take tranquil-lizers or analgesics. They can be life-saving and they improve the quality of life for many. If you are going to use drugs, be well informed about what they are, what they do and what side-effects they have. All drugs have side-effects. Work in partnership with your doctor. If they do not know, look up the information in the standard medical references available at the local library. Make sure you get an answer to the important question 'How will I know when this medication is no longer necessary?'

SOMATIC PACING

Pain may be the last signal before illness or the first signal of illness. How should you react?

In practice we tend to react in one of two ways: quench the pain with an analgesic drug or ignore it. Trying to ignore pain does not work. The more you try not to think about it, the more you focus on it and the more you are caught in it. Rather, get involved in another activity. It is miraculous sometimes how aches and pains disappear as soon as we do something we enjoy. When we are deeply involved in something, we do not notice pain. For example athletes will finish a game and only realize the extent of their injuries afterwards. Before you become involved in another activ-ity, though, respect the pain as a signal that needs your attention.

First how *not* to give it attention.

A pain begins, for example a headache. It rates 1 out of 10 on your personal pain scale. You become alarmed and uneasy. You worry about the pain, wondering whether it will get worse. The worry and suggestion that it will get worse makes it worse. It moves up a notch to a 2. Fear and anxiety release adrenaline which heightens the strength of nerve transmissions. The pain is boosted, perhaps to a 4 out of 10. This can set off a vicious circle and the pain spirals. Then the next time a headache starts, you think, 'I hope it will not be as bad as last time.' This sets the spiral in motion again.

Instead of being caught in this spiral, simply give pain your attention as a sensation in the present moment. Stay away from past experience and future expectation. The act of paying atten-tion will change your experience of pain in subtle ways. Ian has developed this process and calls it 'somatic pacing'. The intention is to acknowledge your experience of pain and discomfort, and by doing so, allow it to evolve.

Instead of trying to get away from the sensation, actually give it your attention. As you do this, notice what happens to the original sensation. It will almost certainly begin to change.

By paying attention to the pain, you change your relationship to the sensation – you begin to be able to influence it directly. Take the worst case, supposing the pain intensified – you now know that you can affect it. Your outcome will be to affect it in the way you want.

You will become aware that although pain is part of your experience, it is not your whole experience. As the person who experiences, you are more than it. You can also address the symptom directly – ask it what its message is for you. It is remarkable how frequently people get an answer that they know is important.

After this there are many other things you can do. One that has proved very useful is to create your personal pain scale. For example:

0   is pain free
1   discomfort
2   painful
3   moderately painful
4   very painful
5   the worst pain you have ever suffered

Grade the intensity of the sensation. The scale can have as many points as you wish. What is important is that they make sense to you. Even thinking about what they might be will make you more discriminating about your own experience.

Grade your level of pain on the scale.

Become curious about it.

Notice the submodalities of the pain.

Where is it located?

How intense is it?

How hot is it?

How large is it?

What area does it cover?

If the pain were to convert to a sound what would that sound be?

If the pain were to convert to a colour, what colour would it be?

This is pacing yourself – somatic pacing. It will change your experience. It may relieve the pain. Now you can lead yourself into another experience.

Take the sound of the pain and listen to it internally. Now change that sound gradually. Notice how changing the sound changes your experience of the pain. Experiment with different sounds. You may be able to completely change the sound to one of comfort by reducing the volume and the rhythm, making it more musical or softer, or changing the direction.

You can also work with the picture, changing the brightness, intensity and colour. Notice how that changes the pain. Different colours will produce different sensations. Find the one that is best for you. When you are working with visual and auditory submodalities, do not make big changes immediately, but explore the effect of changing submodalities gradually. Frequently, just attending without doing sound or colour conversions is enough to allow a process of change to occur.

METAPHORS OF PAIN

Our metaphors of pain influence our experience of it.

Explore the way you think about physical and emotional pain with these questions:

'When I am in pain I can't...'
'What frightens me about pain is...'
'It is OK to groan or scream with pain when...'
'It is not OK to groan and scream with pain when...'
'I admit I am in pain when...'
'I do not admit I am in pain when...'
'The worst pain I have ever felt was...'
'I normally deal with pain by...'
'I have never dealt with pain by...'

You can use the following questions to explore a pain that you are suffering or your experience of pain in general:

PAIN IS LIKE...

BECAUSE...

You do not have to stop at one answer. You will probably find many metaphors.

What does this tell you about how you experience pain?

What else has to be true about pain for your metaphor to be true?

Pain is a communication from your body. Your body does not have words, only sensations. To understand and act on the message, you may need to translate it into words, then the pain may have served its purpose. Use these questions and those following to explore the message. Do not try to force the answers to make sense. Take whatever answers come, however bizarre they appear at first glance.

Take a particular pain or symptom you suffer and finish this sentence:

WHEN I HAVE THIS PAIN I FEEL...

BECAUSE...

Do not limit yourself to just one answer. Let all your negative feelings emerge about the pain.

Pain may also have a positive intention – it is doing something for you, allowing you to achieve something.

Ask yourself this question and write down the answers you get:

WHEN I HAVE THIS PAIN I FEEL RELIEVED
BECAUSE...

Look at your answers. How could this be true? A positive intention nearly always emerges. The pain does help you achieve an outcome you want.

Is there another, better way you could achieve the same outcome without having pain?

SLEEPWALKING INTO ILLNESS

Often we ignore pain – perhaps not wanting to take drugs, perhaps not wanting to make a fuss, just hoping it will go away. But ignoring pain also ignores the message it is trying to give. We risk sleepwalking into illness if we repeatedly ignore the same message. Eventually the messenger will do more to gain our attention than just plucking at our sleeve.

Joseph used to teach full time and it was important for him to work during the school term because that was the only time he could earn money. School terms are about three months long, with a half term holiday in the middle. He would ignore illness during term time and continue to work if possible, but would regularly have a bad cold or be bedridden with 'flu during the holidays. It was as if all the accumulated stress descended in the holidays, when suddenly it was alright to be ill.

In general we take our bodies for granted until they do not work. We also become used to certain ways of being. When you are more aware of your body, you will be more receptive to feedback before it becomes overtly painful. And you will increase your sensitivity to physical pleasure.

Pace yourself to begin with.
What parts of your body are you most usually aware of?
Shade them in the diagram below.
Now, what areas of your body are you dissatisfied with? (Either because they cause you pain, or you are uncomfortable about them, or you feel they are not attractive.)
Shade them in a different colour.
Finally, what parts of your body do you like?
Shade them in another colour.
What do these figures tell you about how you experience your body?

PERSONAL HEALTH SCAN

We have been considering pain. Now we will move through awareness into pleasure, so you may like to change state before reading on by getting up and moving your body.

Your Body Images

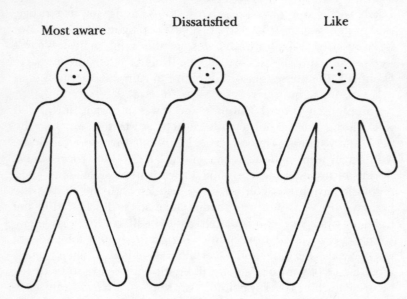

The body scan is a powerful way of increasing your sensitivity and awareness of your body.

Find a quiet place where you can relax for 10 minutes and lie down. Let your attention be drawn into your body. Imagine you are breathing into different parts of your body.

Start in the toes of one foot and move slowly up the foot and leg. When you reach the pelvis, repeat the process down the right leg. Then go back to the pelvis, move up through the torso through the lower back and abdomen, across the upper back and into the chest and shoulders.

Next, go to the fingers of the left hand and move up the arm until you reach the shoulder. Repeat the process for the right arm. Finally, move through the throat and neck, all parts of the face and finish at the top of your head.

It actually does not matter where you start or finish as long as you cover the whole body, feeling each part, internal and external. Feel the heart, the lungs, the digestive system. Do not be content to stay on the surface of the body. Breathe into each region and out from each region.

Let any discomfort or fatigue flow out of your body with the out breath and imagine breathing energy or light into your body with the in breath. Look for areas of health in your body. Draw your own diagram and shade in those areas of health. You may find them in unlikely spots as well as obvious places: in your toes, in the palms of your hands, your lungs, your eyelids or the backs of your knees. You may feel little or nothing in some areas. Others may be painful. Do not let these take your attention until they have their turn, then move fully through them just like the rest.

This is a simple exercise and takes about 10 minutes. There are many relaxation tapes that you can buy to help this process, but the best relaxation tape for you is likely to be the one you make yourself. You will know exactly what to say in exactly the tonality to relax you.

The body scan is one way of being in the present moment and of increasing your awareness of your body. The quality of attention you bring and the willingness to feel whatever there is to feel are more important than breathing the tension from your body.

MEDITATION

The body scan is like meditation. Meditation is sometimes taken as an esoteric discipline coming from Eastern religions, but the word 'meditation' comes from the same root as the word 'medicine'. Both mean measure and balance. We believe some kind of regular meditation is central to health.

There are many forms of meditation. They all involve balancing the mind, body and spirit by being aware in the present moment. Transcendental Meditation (TM) has been widely available in the Western world for over 25 years and has been the subject of intense scientific scrutiny. All systems of relaxation and meditation bring benefits, but the benefits of TM have been the best studied and validated.[2] During TM your breathing rate drops to about 11 times per minute, rather than the usual 16 or 20. Your heart rate slows by at least three beats per minute and your blood pressure decreases. Your galvanic skin resistance

2 *For full reports on the studies, see* Wallace, R., *The Neurophysiology of Enlightenment*, Maharishi International University Press, 1991

(GSR), which is the normal measurement of anxiety, used both in biofeedback and lie detector tests, is some 300 times higher than normal, showing that anxiety and stress are at a minimum. Blood flow to the brain increases by 25 per cent. Even the electrical activity of your brain changes. Brain waves become more synchronized and homogeneous and the alpha waves which are associated with a feeling of relaxation and well-being increase in frequency. You cannot consciously 'will' these things. They happen naturally as a result of meditating. Some of the effects seem to involve balancing the two branches of the autonomic nervous system, allowing a way for thought and action to arise from stillness.

PLEASURE

Which brings us to pleasure. Pleasure is a sign of congruence, the opposite of power. We have no power over pleasure and we cannot fake it, at least not to ourselves. Pleasure seems to be nature's way of reinforcing what is healthy. Everyone has an internal compass that is attracted to health and pleasure is magnetic north. We believe that creating pleasure, loving pleasure and seeking pleasure are healthy. So it is strange how much information there is about the hazards of pleasure and how little about the health benefits.

Pleasure is also something you do for yourself, it is self-affirming and builds your sense of self, particularly if you have been used to working for and paying attention to the needs of others at the expense of your own.

We are born for pleasure. As babies we seek pleasure in order to survive. We can learn to find pleasure in almost anything, even things that are initially painful. We also learn that civilization means forgoing some pleasures, delaying others and discovering more. Yet there is pleasure too in delaying gratification. We can share pleasure and many of the greatest pleasures are shared with others, yet the work ethic and the socialization we endure sets work against pleasure as if the two were contradictory. Some work is boring and unpleasant, but not all. Work is such a central part of our lives that it is surely important to our health that we take as much pleasure in it as possible. Imagine what it is like to do work you love and are congruent about.

The vocabulary of pleasure is limited. We have more distinctions for pain, perhaps because we complain of it, it needs to be described to the doctor and is often the basis of a diagnosis. We do not have to describe pleasure to anyone, let alone complain about it!

SENSUAL PLEASURE

There are many forms of pleasure, but all come directly or indirectly through the senses. We need to see the words to take pleasure in reading, hear the sounds to appreciate the music. Our senses are extraordinarily acute. A candle 10 miles away will stimulate the eye. Our range of hearing spans 10 octaves – between 16 and 20,000 cycles per second. We can smell some chemicals in portions smaller than one million millionths of an ounce. We taste bitterness in one part in two million. Touch can be languid or electrifying. It can convey so much about love, caring and relationship. Sex is one of life's great pleasures. We feel better after good sex. It brings together and satisfies the many needs we have of touch, caring and emotional closeness.

How can you increase your pleasure? One way is to develop your senses. Seek out sights and sounds that give you pleasure. What we see and hear does affect us even when we are not paying very much attention to it. Music influences the respiratory rate, blood pressure, stomach contractions and levels of stress hormones in the blood.[3] There is pleasure and relaxation in watching nature. There is a universe of pleasure in taste and smell. When we develop our senses, we become more acute, we are able to see more, hear more, be more sensitive to taste, touch and smell. We will make finer distinctions in our senses. By learning to make finer distinctions on the outside, we will also be able to make finer distinctions in the representational systems in our mental world. Sensory acuity increases thinking skills. As infants we learned to think through our senses in just such a way. We can make this a lifelong way of learning.

Not only does pleasure come from the senses, but inadequate sense stimulation can even be fatal. Touch is the first sense to

3   Rosenfeld, A., 'Music, the beautiful disturber', *Psychology Today*, December 1985

develop and if it did not feel good, there would be no parenthood and no survival. During the early twentieth century babies were sent to be looked after in an institution when separated from their parents. These infants were not touched or cuddled for fear of infectious diseases. In 1915 a study revealed that nearly every child under two died in these institutions, even though nutrition and sanitation were adequate. Touch is a vital nutrient. The sense of touch not only gives great pleasure, but is essential to our well-being. Infants who are not stimulated with sights and sounds do not thrive or develop as much as those who have a stimulating sensory environment.

Sensual pleasure is all around. Perhaps we have become too serious about pleasure, relegating it to special times and places, and become blind and deaf to many possibilities. We have become too serious about our play. Ian was in an art gallery a few years ago. There was a huge window looking west and through it shone the most magnificent sunset in swirling, changing colours. Inside the gallery was a picture of just such a sunset, probably painted from life. People were admiring the picture – and rightly so, it was good. But they did not notice the real thing that was blazing down on them.

PLEASURE AND HAPPINESS

Pleasure adds to our happiness. Happiness comes partly from narrowing the distance between where you are, your present state, and where you want to be, your desired state. Part of being happy is setting outcomes and moving towards them. We seek difference and diversity. We also need the comfort of the familiar and the repetitive. Happiness seems to be a balance between comforting solace and our insatiable urge for new challenges. Part of the art of being happy is what you keep stable in your life and what you seek to change. Too much stability stifles, too much change overwhelms. We can argue that the four pillars of NLP are the basis of pleasure and happiness in life – rapport and relationship, setting and achieving outcomes, developing the senses, sensory acuity and the flexibility of choice so you are never stuck.

There are three main ways to miss happiness. One is to be continually dissociated, knowing a lot about happiness in the abstract, but hardly ever experiencing it. To get pleasure from experience and be happy you need to associate, to be in time. The second way to miss happiness is to treat it as something to be pursued, something elusive outside us that we must chase. The word 'happiness' is a another nominalization. You cannot possess it, you have to create it moment by moment. The third way to miss happiness is to think it must be a great event, a momentous occasion, and in looking for these, miss the small daily pleasures that add up to a healthy and happy life. Happiness is not only in the peaks but in the whole mountain range.

How happy are you right now?

Please mark your Personal Happiness Rating on the scale:

Very unhappy   Very happy

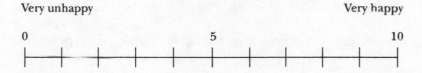

Personal happiness rating

Happiness is completely subjective, so there can be no comparison with others.

Now think of the most wonderful experience that could happen to you, perhaps winning the lottery. Where would you put your score now?

Now think of the worst thing that could happen to you while still alive, perhaps a crippling accident. Where would you put your score now?

You may be interested in the results of some surveys in response to these questions. The average happiness rating was found to be 6.5. A survey of paraplegics gave an average rating of 6.0, a mere 0.5 difference. A lottery win did originally push the scale up to 9 or 10, but one year later the self-reported rating of the lottery winners was back at about 6.5.[4] They were hardly happier a year later and it is also interesting that they reported much less pleasure in their daily activities, relationships and work. Why? Because we adapt. We upgrade our expectations based on our circumstances. The more

4 Brickman, P., 'Adaptation level determinants of satisfaction with equal and unequal outcome distributions in skill and change situations', *Journal of Personality and Social Psychology* 32 (1975), 191–8

you have, the more you take for granted and the more you need to make a difference. Happiness is based on the comparison of what you have, whatever level that may be, with what you want.

DAILY PLEASURE RATING

Are you getting a sufficient supply of day-to-day pleasure?

We do not plan to give pleasure prescriptions, but for you to do more of what gives you pleasure and to get more from it. What do you do frequently that you really enjoy?

And are you getting the most from it?

Think of the many enjoyable experiences you have had in the past.

Make a list of at least three and up to five pleasant experiences under each of these headings:

1 open air
2 professional
3 sport
4 music
5 hobbies
6 travel
7 relationships, friends and family
8 reading
9 children
10 sex
11 religious and spiritual activity
12 clothes
13 problem solving
14 financial
15 cooking
16 friends
17 television
18 holidays
19 games
20 random acts of kindness

For example, the first heading is the open air. Five occasions of taking pleasure might be a walk after dinner, seeing a sunset, watching snow fall, listening to birdsong and smelling new mown grass. Five examples from the second heading might be being promoted, solving a problem at work, meeting friends, having your work praised and praising others. Random acts of kindness covers those times when you have been kind to others with absolutely no justification or others have been kind to you unexpectedly. We are used to reading of random acts of violence – why not random acts of kindness?

If it is difficult to fill a category, you may be thinking in too grandiose terms. These pleasures can be as simple and short as you wish – the first mouthful of lunch, the languid moments before fully waking, listening to children playing – if you were there to enjoy them.

Another approach would be to go over the last few months and remember pleasures and then place them in a category.

Which of these experiences do you take the greatest pleasure in?

Which give you the greatest self-esteem?

What pleasures are not yet on your list that you would like to be?

Twenty headings with five examples each makes a total of 100.

Now think back over the last month. You may have done some things several times. Score each item as follows:

1 You took little pleasure in it.
2 You quite enjoyed it.
3 You really enjoyed it.

There is a top score of 300 points. What is your score? Divide it by 30 for your daily pleasure rating.

DAILY PLEASURE RATING (DPR)...
Is it enough? Can you do better next month?

Do not forget laughter. We often think laughter is a reaction to pleasure, yet it is a pleasure in itself. The scientific definition of a laugh is: 'A psychophysiological reflex, a successive, rhythmic, spasmodic, expiration with open glottis and vibration of the vocal chords, often accompanied by a baring of the teeth and facial grimaces.'[5] A grim description, worth a chuckle in itself. There is

5 Brodie, R., 'Anatomy of a laugh', *American Health*, November/December 1983, 42–7

evidence that laughter boosts the immune system[6] and it raises pain thresholds.[7] There is evidence too that humour and laughter decrease levels of the stress hormones epinephrine and cortisol.[8] We really must take humour more seriously.

Finally, and fittingly, to end this chapter, think of the pleasures of sleep. When we are sleepy enough, we will forego almost any other pleasure in favour of sleep. We do not understand it, but we need it and anything we need to do, nature makes a pleasure.

The brain cannot relax outside sleep and even within sleep it shuffles its deck of experiences, presenting us with our ration of nocturnal metaphors like a mad raconteur to keep us sane. The body uses the time to repair itself. There is a link between sleep and the immune system – a variety of chemicals are released in deep sleep that are known to wake the immune system into action.[9] Perhaps that is why we sleep more when we are ill. There is also evidence that sleep protects health. A study of 5,000 adults over nine years showed that those subjects that slept seven to eight hours a night had the lowest death rates from heart disease, cancer and stroke. The short sleepers (six hours or less) and the long sleepers (nine hours or more) were 30 per cent more likely to die prematurely. The study did not distinguish between natural sleep and sleep forced by circumstances, but the statistics are suggestive.[10]

Sleep is part of the natural rhythm of our lives that pervades all we do. There are the larger rhythms of the year, the turn of the seasons and the natural waking–sleep rhythm of day and night. There are also smaller rhythms within the day. These ultradian rhythms give the natural ebb and flow we experience in

6   Dillon, K., Minchoff, B., and Baker, K., 'Positive emotional states and enhancement of the immune system', *International Journal of Psychiatry in Medicine* 15 (1985), 13–17

7   Cogan, R., Cogan, D., Waltz, W., and McCue, M., 'Effects of laughter and relaxation on discomfort thresholds', *Journal of Behavioural Medicine* 10 (2) (1987), 139–44

8   Berk, L. *et al.*, 'Laughter decreases cortisol, epinephrine and 3,4-dihydroxyphenyl acetic acid (DOPAC) abstract', *Journal of the Society of Behavioural Medicine* (1988)

9   Krueger, J., Karnovsky, M., 'Sleep and the immune response', *Annals of the New York Academy of Science* 496 (1987), 510–16

10 Wingard, D., and Berkman, L., 'Mortality risk associated with sleeping patterns among adults', *Sleep* 6 (2) (1983), 102–7

the day and night. Every 90 minutes during sleep, most people experience a period of dreaming shown by rapid eye movement.[11]

Further research has found a one and a half to two hour rhythm of rest followed by activity, linked to dominance of the left or right hemisphere of the brain.[12] These rhythms seem to be modulated by the autonomic and endocrine systems. Even individual cells have metabolic high and low activity points during the day. One way that cancer cells show they are unnatural is that they invert this rhythm, showing the greatest activity when normal cells are showing the least, a fact that is utilized in the timing of radiation and chemotherapy in cancer treatment.

We seriously disrupt these natural rhythms at our peril. Stress will disturb them and many researchers link this to illness and stress disorders.[13]

When you are feeling tired or irritable during the day, you may need to take a short break, a time to daydream, relax, meditate or even take a short sleep. These natural rhythms are truly part of our biological self. Pacing them is part of pacing ourselves.

FOOD FOR THOUGHT

In theory, there should not be much difference between theory and practice; but in practice, there often is.

Anon

...may God us keep
from single vision and Newton's sleep

William Blake

11 Goldstein, L., Stoltzfus, L., and Gardocki, J., 'Changes in interhemispheric amplitude relationships in EEG during sleep', *Physiology and Behaviour* 8 (1972), 811–15

12 Klein, R., and Armitage, R., 'Rhythms in human performance: one and a half hour alterations in cognitive style', *Science* 204 (1979), 1326–8

13 Friedman, S., 'A psychophysiological model for the chemotherapy of psychosomatic illness', *Journal of Nervous and Mental Diseases* 166 (1978), 110–16

see also Friedman, S., Kantor, I., Sobel, S., and Miller, R., 'On the treatment of neurodermatitis with monomine oxidase inhibition 66', *Journal of Nervous and Mental Diseases* 166 (1978), 117–25

Human feelings are words expressed in human flesh.

Aristotle

You grow up on the day you have the first real laugh at yourself.

Ethel Barrymore

Healing is a matter of time, but it is sometimes a matter of opportunity.

Hippocrates

The great secret of doctors known only to their wives, but still hidden from the public is that most things get better by themselves, most things in fact are better in the morning.

Dr Lewis Thomas, President, Memorial Sloan Kettering Institute for Cancer Research

The brain is my second favourite organ.

Woody Allen

Sleep ... balm of hurt minds, great nature's second course; chief nourisher in life's feast.

William Shakespeare, *Macbeth*

11

HEALTHY AGEING

Ageing seems the only way available to live a long time.

Daniel François Esprit Auber

How long do you want to live? Living a long time means you age. Time's winged chariot hurries on in one direction only, despite our best efforts, but we age in different ways and at different rates.

Although medicine has vastly increased our average life expectancy, the maximum does not seem to have changed in recorded history. In 1996, a lady who lives in Paris has reached the highest substantiated age on record – 120 years old.

What does old age mean to you? If it conjures up the spectres of illness, frailty, loss of mental powers and decreasing quality of life, then long life is not a very inviting proposition. Healthy ageing is what we seek and that is different from just not dying. It is having a good quality and quantity of life. The ideal is to die as young as possible as late as possible.

In 1995 a report by the United Kingdom Office of Population Censuses and Surveys stated that at the age of 65, women can expect to live another 18 years and men another 13, but they are likely to enjoy good health for only half those years. Medicine may give us extra years, but they are not necessarily healthy ones. A long and healthy life is something you have to create for yourself.

Western culture exhibits spectacular incongruence about growing old. There is fear of ageing and prejudice against the old. Youth is the ideal and 'young' is equivalent to 'attractive'. If you cannot be young then at least you must look young. Different standards are applied to men and women. Older women are judged more harshly. More store is put on a woman's physical attractiveness than a man's. In this culture, 'old' equals 'unattractive, unhealthy and unfit'. It is this vicious triumvirate that we fear rather than age itself.

NLP can make two positive contributions. The first is to model healthy ageing. What are the qualities of those people who age in a healthy way, living long, active and happy lives? The second is to tease out the negative beliefs and presuppositions that prevent healthy ageing.

THE THREE AGES

In the myth of Oedipus, the Sphinx asked every passing traveller the same question: 'What animal has four legs in the morning, two in the afternoon and three in the evening?' Those who did not answer were killed. Oedipus gave the right answer – a man – crawling in the morning of life, walking in the prime of life and using a walking stick for support in old age. These were known as the three ages of man.

Now we think of people having three ages however old they are:

• chronological age
• biological age
• psychological age

Chronological age is the number of years you have been alive measured by the calendar.

Biological age is the wear and tear on your body. This is what causes biological ageing and all the physical changes that we associate with age. Eventually the accumulated damage is fatal.

Psychological age is how old you feel, how you think, and the quality of the emotional and intellectual life you enjoy.

These three are interdependent but not the same. We judge age solely by chronological age, yet this is misleading. What of the 30 year old whose habits have given him the heart and lungs of a person of 50? What of the 50 year old who has more energy than her 20-year-old colleagues? What of the 20 year old who is so set in his ways as to make an octogenarian look adventurous? The three ages do not stay in step. Only chronological age marches steadily and inexorably as the seasons turn. The others may keep pace, run ahead or lag behind. If it is possible for some people to live to 110 in chronological age, then it is arguable that for many people biological and psychological age run ahead of chronological age by 20 years or more.

The interdependence of psychological and biological was wonderfully demonstrated in 1979 by Ellen Langer and her colleagues at Harvard. They studied a group of men, all aged 75 or over, for a week at a country resort. This was a holiday with a difference. The resort was set up as if it were 20 years in the past. Magazines and newspapers were from 1959, not 1979. The music was from 1959. The men were asked to behave as if it were 1959 and talk of events of that year in the present tense. All the men were retired, but they were asked to speak of their jobs as if they were employed 20 years earlier. They all wore identification photographs of themselves taken 20 years before. During the study, the research team took measurements of the subjects' biological age as shown by such markers as strength, short-term memory, and acuity of hearing, sight and taste.

The physical results of this mental time travel were remarkable. The group was judged by impartial observers to look an average of three years younger judged from their photographs after the study. Finger length tends to shorten with age, but the fingers of this group had lengthened. Stiff joints were more flexible. Many of the men became more active and self-sufficient, whereas before they had relied on younger family members to look after them. Muscle strength improved, as did hearing and eyesight. Over half the group showed an increase in intelligence during the study, measured by standard tests. The control group did not show any of these improvements to the same degree.

The minds of these men were taken back 20 years and their bodies had followed. Langer thought the success of this experiment was due to the men behaving as if they were younger, being treated as if they were younger and being asked to follow more complex daily instructions than they were used to.

What do these results suggest?

First, that psychological and biological age affect each other and they are not a one-way trip like chronological age.

Second, that we live to a great extent by what is expected of us. Old people are often treated as if they are less intelligent and able. They then live up (or down) to these expectations.

Lastly, it demonstrates the power of anchors. They profoundly affect our physical and mental state.

BIOLOGICAL AGE

Ageing is a gradual and complex process. We do not know how or why it takes place. One theory emphasizes hereditary and genetic factors. The other emphasizes the wear and tear suffered by the body in the course of living. The truth may be somewhere between the two. Time reduces the efficiency in all our bodily systems, but does not destroy it.

The body does not age at a constant rate. Stress ages it more quickly. Also different parts of the body age at different rates. Most people have a 'weak spot' that causes trouble and where they first feel the effect of stress.

From the moment of conception there is a balance in the body between tissue being destroyed and tissue repair. The rate of ageing depends on this relationship. At the end of a year, over 98 per cent of the atoms in your body will be new. Somehow the wisdom of the body manages this beautiful and complex process. It faithfully reproduces the body we create for ourselves. As time passes, though, the rate of tissue damage increases, or perhaps our bodies become less adept at repairing the damage. Poorly repaired tissue works less efficiently and is more likely to degenerate further. Damage accumulates like a snowball rolling downhill.

The damage is caused by toxins, environmental agents, pollutants, background radiation, both solar and industrial, disease and the normal processes of metabolism that produce breakdown products that can damage cells. The most important of these breakdown products are free radicals and aldehydes. Free radicals are very reactive molecules that are produced naturally in our bodies and have the potential to do a lot of damage at the cellular level. There is now a huge amount of research which suggests that free radical scavengers such as vitamin C and vitamin E can have a critical role in neutralizing these molecules and so slow ageing.[1]

1   *See* Sharma, H., *Freedom from Disease*, Maharishi International University Press, 1994

PSYCHOLOGICAL AGE

Our minds influence every cell in our bodies, so human ageing is fluid. It can speed up, slow down, stop or even go into reverse, as the Harvard experiments showed. Our beliefs and expectations influence how we age. What beliefs do you have about ageing?

Let us start with your metaphor:

Ageing is like...

Because...

What does this tell you about how you view ageing?

There are a number of myths about ageing in Western culture that still hold sway despite numerous counter examples.

The first is that old age begins at 65. At that point your active life is presumed to be over. From then on it's a gentle slide into inactivity. Men retire at 65, the argument goes, because they are too old for work. In fact, 65 is an arbitrary age. It was originally fixed as retirement age for political reasons. Germany established the world's first state social security system in 1889. Bismarck, the chancellor at the time, picked 70 as the official retirement age and it was later reduced to 65 by officialdom. Life expectancy in Germany at the time was 45. Retirement age was therefore 56 per cent higher than life expectancy. If today's retirement age were picked by such criteria, we would be retiring at 117.

Retirement age is a vestige of the old linear life plan where you learned, pursued your career, then retired and died. The changing nature of work and the fact that we are all living longer makes this plan obsolete. Why have all the leisure time bunched towards the end and all the learning at the beginning? A cyclic and more flexible life plan makes more sense, learning, working and relaxing in stages throughout life.

Nor has it ever been proved that older people are less productive. There have been many studies of thousands of workers, from semi-skilled workers to managers, and all have shown that apart from a slight decline in productivity in jobs that required great physical effort, older workers performed as well as or better than younger workers.[2] The claim that most creative work was accomplished by people under 50 in the past is answered by the fact that most people did not live past 50.

The second myth about ageing is that decay is inevitable, and that older people are necessarily in poorer health and mentally less bright than younger people. This is not so. Poor health is an issue of lifestyle. Years of sedentary lifestyle and poor nutrition will take their toll. Most of the current problems of old age are preventable or postponable. It is a truism that we lose a million brain cells every year, but we have 10 billion neurons with a million billion connections, so there is hardly cause for alarm. What beliefs do you have about ageing?

Think about the following questions:

What messages did you get about ageing and attractiveness from your mother about men and women?
What messages did you get about ageing and attractiveness from your father about men and women?

The message will come from words and more powerfully from behaviour.

How would you complete the following?

In general, men in their fifties are...
In general, women in their fifties are...
In general, men in their sixties are...
In general, women in their sixties are...
In general, men older than 60 are...
In general, women older than 60 are...

What messages do you get from television and the media about ageing?

2   *See* Robinson, P., 'Research update: the older worker', *Generations,* Summer 1983
see also Schwab, D., and Heneman, H., 'Effects of age and experience on productivity', *Industrial Gerontology* 4 (1977), 2
also US Department of Labour, *The Older American Workers: Age discrimination in employment,* 1965
and US Senate Committee on Human Resources, *Findings on Age, Capacity and Productivity,* 1977

What are your worst fears about ageing?
What actions can you take to make sure these never happen?
What are your best hopes about ageing?
What can you do to ensure that these are realized?
What will it be like to look back and know that these have been realized?

HEALTHY AGEING

There have been many studies on healthy ageing, including an NLP modelling project by Robert Dilts.[3] It will come as no surprise that there is general agreement that all the factors that undermine your health also accelerate the ageing process. Conversely, those things that retard ageing keep you healthy.

The following are the main factors that accelerate biological ageing:

* stress
* worry
* feeling helpless
* depression
* hostility towards self and others
* inability to express emotions
* lack of close friends
* smoking

Job dissatisfaction and financial problems tend to cause the most stress and worry.

By contrast the main factors associated with healthy longevity are:

optimism
hope
a sense of control
happiness

These are all self-rated qualities. Only you can decide.

3 Dilts, R., and Hollander, J., *NLP and Life Extension: Modelling longevity*, Dynamic Learning Publications, 1990

Not surprisingly, the above qualities were found to link with financial security and job satisfaction.

happy long-term relationships with friends and spouse
the ability to make and keep close friends
drinking alcohol moderately
exercising moderately and regularly
sleeping six to eight hours a night

Healthy ageing is linked to certain behaviour, ways of thinking and beliefs.

For example, there is evidence that meditation can slow and even reverse biological ageing. Long-term meditators who have been practising TM for more than five years have been found to be physically 12 years younger than their chronological age, as measured by reduction of blood pressure, better near point vision and auditory discrimination. The study controlled for the effects of diet and exercise.[4]

Moderate, frequent exercise is also healthy behaviour. Regular physical exercise can reverse 10 of the most typical effects of physiological age, including high blood pressure, excess body fat, poor blood sugar balance and decreased muscle mass. A sedentary lifestyle has been linked to an increased risk of stroke, coronary heart disease and colon cancer.[5] People who are physically inactive have roughly twice the rate of heart disease and heart attacks as more active people. Inactivity is dangerous.

This message has been repeated until we have become tired of hearing it, especially from government bodies. Many people do not act on it because it seems as if exercise is something special, time-consuming and apart from everyday life. It is quite the opposite. Movement and fitness can be a healthy pleasure, and it needs very little physical activity to achieve many health benefits. In one long-term Harvard study, health benefits began with an expendi-

---

4 Wallace, R., Jacobe, E., and Harrington, E., 'The effects of the Transcendental Meditation and TM-sidhi program on the aging process', *International Journal of Neuroscience* 16 (1) (1982), 53–8

5 *Health Education Authority and Sports Council, Allied Dunbar National Fitness Survey: Main findings*, Sports Council and HEA, 1992
   see also Blair, S. *et al.*, 'Physical fitness and all-cause mortality: a prospective study of healthy men and women', *Journal of the American Medical Association* 262 (1989), 2395–401

ture of only 500 calories a week – achieved by one 15-minute walk each day.[6]

About half an hour of moderate exercise three to five times a week is all that is needed. That exercise can be anything you like – gardening, walking, housework or swimming. Doing anything physical is better than remaining inactive.

The other reason people do not exercise is that health is confused with fitness. Fitness is the capacity to take in and utilize oxygen and make greater physical effort. It is also muscle strength, stamina and flexibility. It is possible to be fit and not healthy, and also possible to be healthy but not very fit. Beware of damaging your health in the pursuit of fitness. *Moderate, regular exercise* is healthy. Strenuous exercise builds fitness and a better quality of life, but does not add to the length of your life.

There is no doubt that weight is also important to health, although there is still a great deal of uncertainty as to precisely how it affects it. Western culture is obsessed with weight and has turned it into a major health and identity issue. Being seriously overweight or underweight is dangerous, but a normal, healthy weight will vary from person to person.

Nutrition and diet are controversial; there have been many conflicting reports and different recommendations come and go. However, maintaining a reasonably steady weight seems to be important. A study of Harvard Graduates from 1962 to 1988 showed that those who gained or lost substantial weight (11 pounds or over) were at greater risk, which suggests that each person does have a natural weight that the body seeks to maintain.

Obesity is not the same as weight. Obesity is an excessive accumulation of fat beyond what is considered normal for age, sex and body type, and is defined as more than 20 per cent fat for men and more than 30 per cent fat for women. These are arbitrary levels. Set them low enough and everyone in the world would be defined as obese. It is possible to be underweight and still obese.

Our preoccupation with weight and how important it is to self-image fuels a huge diet industry. A strange message is implied: the more you weigh, the less healthy you are. This is not true, although there is no doubt that beyond a certain point, different

6 Paffenenbarger, R., Hyde, R., Wing, W. *et al.*, 'Physical activity, all-cause mortality and longevity of college alumni', *New England Journal of Medicine* March 314 (1986), 605–13

for each of us, excess weight is a health hazard, putting extra strain on the heart and the musculo-skeletal joints.

A balanced diet needs to be psychologically satisfying and give a balanced supply of nutrients appropriate to your physiology each day. But nutrition has been hijacked into maintaining a culturally defined desirable weight.

Fear of fat is often more about appearance than about health. The cultural preoccupation with fat means many people diet who do not need to. Dieting seems so simple – eat less – lose weight – go back to normal eating and maintain the new weight. However, it does not work that way. In the long run most diets are ineffective and dieters gain weight. So they diet again. This can become a repetitive cycle. Dieting to lose weight is the perfect example of not treating the body as a natural, complex, self-organizing system.

When you stop a diet, you gain weight more easily for three reasons:

• The initial weight loss is not fat, but a mixture of glycogen (a form of glucose stored in the muscles and liver and which is the most immediately available for energy) and water. Lack of glycogen causes low blood sugar levels which can result in depression, tiredness and irritability. Low glycogen levels result in reduced energy expenditure and a slowing of the metabolic rate as your body becomes more efficient at using food. It stays at this lower rate for some time afterwards, so you gain weight more easily. Exercise while dieting can reverse this metabolic slowing.

• Dieting makes your body more efficient at storing fat, which makes it easier to gain weight afterwards.

• After glycogen, the body loses the tissue it needs least. If you are sedentary, this is lean muscle tissue that normally burns unwanted calories. When you return to former eating habits, the body cannot burn so many calories, so you are likely to gain weight and fat beyond previous levels. Exercise is the only way to minimize the loss of lean tissue while dieting. Studies of weight loss have shown that even after four years the body is still trying to return to its initial weight.[7]

Most of what we have said about healthy ageing is well known and

7   *British Medical Journal* 310, 18 March 1995, 750

has been published in newspapers and magazines. The facts are easy to establish. If knowing the facts were enough, we would all be more healthy. To put them into practice we need the capability – the how to – and the beliefs to overcome personal obstacles.

NLP can help here, for we can use it in practical ways to reduce stress and worry, reframe experience and generalize in a way that supports our health. We can build and maintain good relationships through rapport skills. NLP opens our eyes to the limiting beliefs and metaphors we have about health and ageing. We can use it to build a compelling personal future by setting outcomes and building timelines. How long is your timeline? How long do you want it to be? Visualizing a healthy future and a long timeline is the first step to creating it.

As already mentioned, unhealthy habits may be hard to give up because they hold something of value. Keep what is of value, but achieve it another way, a way that is congruent with your overall health and values. Incongruence is the result of different parts of us pursuing different outcomes in different ways. For example, one part of us wants to exercise, but another does not. One part wants to reduce the hours of work, but another wants to work longer hours to earn more money. Incongruence is like a personal civil war and the result may be stalemate. Congruence comes from knowing what you want and what is important to you, and taking action to achieve it in ways that embody those same important values.

As we go through life we metabolize experience. We wear our lives and our expectations on our faces and throughout our bodies. We embody our models of the world. We are shaped by our experiences and shape them in turn. Change your experience and you change your biological age.

FOOD FOR THOUGHT

Man fools himself – he prays for a long life and he fears an old age.

Chinese proverb

What makes old age so hard to bear is not the failing of one's faculties, mental and physical, but the burden of one's memories.

W. Somerset Maugham

The probability of dying doubles every eight years after puberty.

Gompertz Law

After 70, if you wake without any pains at all, you're dead.

Malcolm Cowley, 'About Men: Being Old', *New York Times* magazine, 26 May 1985

We may invent the elixir of immortality, but it will take forever to prove it.

Anon

The utility of living consists not in the length of days, but in the use of time; a man may have lived long, and yet lived but a little.

Montaigne

DEATH

Oh Lord, give each of us his own death.

Rainer Maria Rilke

At birth we inhale our first breath and at death we exhale our last; the cycle is complete. However many years we live, death is the end of this life's journey, the door back into the mystery from which we emerge. Although it may seem strange to devote a chapter to death in a book on health, we cannot ignore it, because death is a part of life. The actor cannot give a good performance if the curtain never falls, an athlete cannot set a time without a finishing tape, and a musician could not shape a performance without a finale. Despite the hopes of cryogenics and the speculations of nanotechnology, there is always an end.

Yet death gives meaning to life. There is a limited time to do things and this creates the urgency to do them. One way to find out your most vital task in life is to ask yourself, 'If I were to die tomorrow, what is the thing I would most regret not having accomplished?' Are you content to die with that unaccomplished?

As we age, we have the opportunity to become more ourselves and death can be another expression of the same self, not a random, meaningless event to be feared. We are unique in life and we will be unique in death.

THE WILL TO LIVE?

Death is one of the few taboo subjects for serious discussion. We deny it. It is even illegal to die of old age – the World Health

Organization does not allow it. Everyone, everywhere in the world, must die of a specific cause. 'Old age' is inadmissible on a death certificate. It is as if life really goes on forever unless accident or disease cuts it short.

Only about one third of the adult population of England has made a will. It is not that people have nothing to leave, but a will is an uncomfortable reminder of your own mortality, as if to think about death might somehow invite it to stalk you. Yet making a will is common sense, it allows your affairs to be settled more quickly and in a less distressing way for friends and family.

As long as we deny death it retains its power to frighten us and we will always be unprepared for it. Another of the consequences of denying death is that we do not learn to say a full and proper goodbye to those we love when they die. We find it hard to deal with loss ourselves and to console those who have lost close friends and family. When there is unfinished business it is difficult to move on and to grieve completely, able to let someone go in the flesh while keeping them alive in your heart.

At the same time death is fascinating. We enjoy it vicariously in films and books. In Japan there are specially licensed chefs who prepare the flesh of the puffer fish. Diners pay large sums of money for this delicacy, which must be prepared with the greatest care because parts of the puffer fish contain tetrodotoxin, one of the most poisonous chemicals in the world. A pinhead of the poison would be fatal if eaten. The danger of *fugu*, as it is called, is well known. This is gastronomic Russian roulette – you eat the possibility of death – and the best chefs try to leave the slightest hint of poison, enough to make your mouth tingle and remind you of your flirtation with death. Indeed, several diners do die in Japan every year. Like Russian roulette, one of the pleasures must be the exquisite relief at the end of the meal that you have survived, you have cheated death, that perhaps, after all, you are immortal.

IS YOUR LIFE KILLING YOU?

How long will you allow yourself to live? Is a long and healthy life one of your important values and what are you prepared to do to create it?

There is a great deal you can do to influence your health and longevity. Are you seeking out environments that nourish you? Are you allowing yourself a healthy balance of rest, relaxation, exercise and laughter? Are you building and maintaining close relationships, establishing a sense of control, hope and optimism? Belief and hope in a long life are necessary but insufficient. They must be backed by action. Do your environment, behaviour, thinking patterns, beliefs and values align towards a long and healthy life? Are you satisfied with the balance of change and stability in your life? Do you have a good balance between paying attention to yourself and your needs and paying attention to others and their needs? What are you doing that is making it harder for your body to serve you well?

This would be a good time to take stock.

Take two sheets of paper.

On the first sheet, list all those ways you could be shortening your life. Be honest and specific.

Use the logical levels to organize them. Start with environment, then go through behaviour, habits and thought patterns, and beliefs.

These are your most important health issues.

On the other sheet of paper, list all those ways, grouped by logical level, that you are lengthening your life. Again, be honest and specific.

These are your most important resources.

Life Shorteners		Life Enhancers
_____	*Identity*	_____
_____		_____
_____		_____
_____	*Beliefs and Values*	_____
_____		_____
_____		_____
_____	*Capabilities*	_____
_____		_____
_____		_____
_____	*Behaviour*	_____
_____		_____
_____		_____
_____	*Environmental Factors*	_____
_____		_____
_____		_____

DEATH AS AN ADVISER

What does death mean to you? There are many metaphors of death. When we think of death, we often see it as darkness, the enemy, the end, something to be kept at bay. Sleep is the most common metaphor. How could death become a resource?

Carlos Castaneda has written at length of Don Juan, a Yaqui Indian mystic.[1] In Don Juan's philosophy, death is an adviser. It grounds you, reminding you that you are part of nature and not above it. Whenever you have a decision to make, you turn and ask death (death waits behind your left shoulder), 'What would you have me do if this were my last act on Earth?'

This is a moving question. It makes you think about what you do. Your last act on Earth has a very special significance. You would want it to be a very powerful expression of who you are. There is also the added poignancy that there is no guarantee that what you decide is not in fact your last act on Earth. With death as an adviser you are reminded to make your next action as congruent and powerful an expression of your identity as possible. And then the next. And the next. Death's tap on the shoulder reminds us to make the most of the present.

Death is a stern adviser and you may prefer another to give you the message. We are not saying you need to be always thinking of death. Obsession with death is as bad as or even worse than denial, but death does have much to teach us.

YOUR LAST ACT ON EARTH

Death *is* your last act on Earth. What kind of death do you want? Could it be the last act of your life's drama, fully expressive of the person you are? In Eastern spiritual traditions, death is a time of transition, just like birth. In Western society we are just beginning to see birth from the baby's and mother's point of view rather than as a medical condition, and make the experience as comfortable and welcoming as possible for both. Could it be so for death, too? There are more important issues than medical technology at the two extremes of life. It seems to us that death is made harder to bear for the dying and for their loved ones and those that care

1   Castaneda, C., *Journey to Ixtlan*, Bodley Head, 1972

for them, unless we accept it for what it is.

The next exercise is best done in a quiet place, lying or sitting down in a relaxed frame of mind.

Just for a few minutes, for the purpose of enriching your life right now, we invite you to take a journey down your timeline into the future, however far that might be, until you reach a point where you cannot or do not wish to do anything more in this life.

Whatever you believe lies beyond that is there in the future, but we invite you to turn around and look back towards now.

As you do so, ask yourself:

What did I want to have accomplished by this point?
What does it feel like to have accomplished these things?
What would it be like *not* to have accomplished those things?
How do my actions back in the present move me towards or away from these things that I want to accomplish?
What advice would I give the me back in the present as I look now from the end of my life?

How important are the worries of your present self from this point of view?
What is the most important thing that your present self needs to do now?
What emotions do you feel as you look back on your present self?

Come back to the present moment and reflect a little on what you have learned.

Now think of how you want that time to be – that time when you cannot or do not wish to do anything more in this life.

The death you want begins with what you do now. You may be carrying mental baggage that weighs you down – unresolved anger, hurt, resentment and guilt. You may want to travel the next part of your timeline more lightly.

The experience of facing death has been divided into a number of stages: first denial, then anger, then bargaining, then depression, then acceptance and finally healing.[2] The healing may

2 Kübler-Ross, E., *On Death and Dying,* Tavistock Publications, 1969

be back into life or may be death itself – the passing into a new state, the end of one way of being. It seems to us that these are stages of life as well. We are always dying to one way of being to enter into another – infancy, childhood, adolescence, adulthood, falling in love, becoming a parent. These are all changes, all little deaths followed by rebirth. You already know much about death from your experience of life.

What comes from these thoughts is to live every day as if it were your last and every day as if it will last forever. The results can be magical.

In the words of a Tibetan proverb: 'It is better to have lived one day as a tiger, than one thousand years as a sheep.'

FOOD FOR THOUGHT

> You die as you have lived. If you were paranoid in life, you will probably be paranoid when you are dying.
> Dr James Cimino, Medical Director, Calvary Hospital, New York Institute
> for the Terminally Ill

> Then Almitra spoke, saying, we would ask now of death.
> And he said:
> You would know the secret of death.
> But how shall you find it unless you seek it in the heart of life?
> Kahlil Gibran, *The Prophet*

> Life does not cease to be fun when people die any more than it ceases to be serious when people laugh.
> George Bernard Shaw

> Certain indeed is death for the born
> and certain is birth for the dead,
> therefore over the inevitable
> Thou shouldst not grieve.
> *Bhagavad Gita* 2:27

> If it be now, 'tis not to come;
> if it be not to come, it will be now;
> if it be not now, yet it will come:
> the readiness is all.
> William Shakespeare, *Hamlet*

13

CONGRUENCE HEALS

> Where love of mankind is, there is also love of the art of medi-
> cine.
>
> Hippocrates, *Precepts*

Finally, a short chapter to pull some of the threads together. The
consumer revolution tempts us to think we are consumers of
health, but we are not, we are its creators – by what we do, how we
think and how we live. Our bodies take in and metabolize not only
air and food, but also time and experience. How we use all these
creates our health from moment to moment. Modern medicine
takes an objective, dissociated view of health. NLP says that you
need also to understand it from the inside. Health and illness are
subjective experiences. Every person's experience and inner world
are different.

REMARKABLE RECOVERIES

The ability to heal is a sign of being alive. What of those cases of
healing on the brink of death, those seemingly miraculous and
remarkable recoveries that have been reported from all times and
places? What can they tell us about healing? NLP is about modelling excellence. It looks at the exceptional, at the limits of human
experience, to understand the powers we all have, but may not
use. How can someone pull back from the brink of death?

One remarkable fact soon emerges: such cases are rarely inves-
tigated. Statistics are often compiled leaving out the 'outliers' –
the extreme ends of the statistical curve, those cases who are so

different from the rest as to make them exceptional. Yet these are precisely the people who hold some intriguing answers.

Sometimes these remarkable recoveries are explained away by saying that the initial diagnosis must have been mistaken, for if the patient recovered, they could not have been as ill as was thought. This is reverse logic that assumes what it sets out to prove.

It is also unusual for doctors to risk their reputations by reporting cases of remarkable recovery due to a psychological method or a medically unorthodox treatment. They are afraid that other patients might delay or forego proper medical care in order to test such methods, so they have to act as if all recovery is due to medical treatment. This is a reasonable and congruent response from doctors who believe in their methods of treatment. However, we think it is not the methods of treatment that hold the key, but the spectacular healing response in the patient, and this can be evoked by any system of therapy.

Indeed, remarkable recoveries happen in all systems of medicine, as well as outside them.[1] They have also occurred at religious shrines such as Lourdes, through special diets and fasting, through healers, prayer, mental imagery and even doing nothing. Some people used a combination of methods. The treatments were as varied as the people who took them.

There is no particular personality style associated with remarkable recoveries, no 'recovery prone personality'. The capacity for recovery is found in all personalities and seems to be about the individual finding the right path for them, not being the 'right sort of person'.

There have been a few documented cases of remarkable recovery, although studies are few and far between. The most revealing studies allow the people concerned to talk about their experience in their own way, rather than have it fitted into pre-existing categories. In these cases the key seems to be *congruence*: the patients found a way that was right for them. Whatever the method they used, they were true to themselves. Often their illness forced them to be deeply true to themselves or die. And that is not to say that death may not also be a way of being true to oneself, but for these people at that time in their lives, it was not. Their illness was the ultimate challenge. These people also blended a particular type of

1   *For a good overview of the subject see* Hirshberg, C., and Barasch, M., *Remarkable Recovery*, Riverhead Books, 1995

acceptance with a fighting spirit. They accepted their disease, but did not accept that it necessarily meant they were going to die. Even in extremis, congruence heals. The greater the health challenge the greater the congruence needed to meet it. People who make remarkable recoveries from life-threatening illness also place themselves in a larger context, they have a feeling of connection with others, a spiritual dimension.

SPIRITUAL HEALTH

Congruence is one aspect of the human longing for wholeness, however we think of it. Body, mind and spirit are inseparable, and this is mirrored in our biological development, for brain and heart come from the same embryo cell. So bodily healing will somehow connect with our mental and spiritual life. If we think of the spiritual as our connection with others and the world beyond our identity, then modern medicine is confirming ancient teaching – you look after your own health best by connecting with others.

Spiritual traditions embody enlightened self-interest and have neurophysiological benefits. One study by the immunologist Jeffrey Levin, of 250 cases where religion or spirituality was linked to health outcomes found that religious involvement did have a protective effect, irrespective of age, gender, nationality or social class.[2] The effect was also independent of any particular religions affiliation.

Harvard psychologist David McClelland carried out a widely reported series of experiments where a group of students were shown a short film of Mother Teresa caring for the sick and dying on the streets of Calcutta.[3] The students showed an increased immune system response indicated by their levels of SIgA (Salivary Immunoglobulin Antigen). This was true whatever the students thought of Mother Teresa. Some said they thought she was a fake and her work was useless, but their immune systems still responded positively. Love and caring affect us at a deep level, regardless of our conscious reaction. (When students were shown

2 Levin, J., 'Religion and health: Is there an association, is it valid and is it causal?', *Social Science and Medicine* 38, 11 (1994), 1478
3 McClelland, D., 'Motivation and immune function in health and disease', paper presented at the meeting of the Society of Behavioural Medicine, March 1985

a film of Attila the Hun their antibody levels dropped!)
McClelland also found that the ability to love and care about
others seems to result in lower levels of stress hormone and a
higher level of helper to suppressor T-Cells, an important balance
in a effective immune system. We may not know how love does
this, but there is strong evidence that it does.

HEALTHY QUESTIONS

When you become ill, there is much that you can do to
heal yourself.

The first step is to pace yourself and establish your
present state. Here are some questions to ask yourself:

What am I feeling?
How do I feel about the state I am in?
How was I before I became sick?
What does this illness mean?
What would I like this illness to mean?
What are my resources to feel well?
What is bad about feeling this way?
What might the advantages be in being ill at this time?
What can I learn from this illness?

CONCLUSIONS

NLP studies the structure of subjective experience. With NLP tools
you can understand and model your own states of health. Your
states, emotions and thoughts directly affect your physical health.
The world you create in your mind is 'real' for the body. You can
change your experience by changing the way you use your senses
on the inside, and design the internal world you want through
your representational systems and submodalities. This gives you
tremendous choice and control over your health. It is impossible
to be a victim. You may not be able to change events, but you can
change how you react to them and so minimize stress.

All of the NLP tools work towards a greater sense of self and
a greater degree of congruence. Pace your own experience.
Use your senses to gain pleasure and to increase your acuity of

thinking. Take time for yourself by relaxing or meditating, knowing that it has health benefits. Be aware of your baseline state as a starting-point for designing one more to your liking. Use rapport skills to build and maintain strong supportive relationships. Use timelines and outcomes to build a future that inspires you.

Look at all the logical levels and how they contribute to your health. What supports your health and what do you want to change? Sometimes it is easiest to change behaviour by changing beliefs and values.

Keep pacing yourself. When you pace yourself, you will have more rapport with your body and with the different parts of yourself, and will also be able to connect with others.

Perfect health and perfect congruence are not possible. The journey is what is important, not the destination. Health is not a rigid perfect state, but one with light and shadows.

Illness is not evidence that you have failed, but rather a way to better health, a better state of balance. It can be a transitional state. Illness may be necessary if your old state was too rigid. There may be two types of healing. One takes you back to the state you were before. Although this often seems desirable, remember that nearly all the elements that contributed to that illness will still be there. In more serious illness, generative healing may be needed – healing that takes us beyond the person we were, the person who was prone to that illness in the first place. Unless this type of healing takes place you will become ill again in the same way. Illness can be a way to better health.

THE 10 WARNING SIGNS OF HEALTH

1   An increased awareness and appreciation of yourself.

2   A tendency to set aside a time each day to relax or meditate.

3   A persistent ability to maintain close relationships.

4   A tendency to adapt to changing conditions.

5   A chronic appetite for physical activity.

6   Acute and chronic attacks of laughter.

7   A compulsion to take pleasure and fun.

8   Repeated bouts of hope and optimism.

9   A chronic condition of caring for your body.

10   Recurrent rejection of worry.

Peak experiences and a sense of going beyond a limited identity are also diagnostic signs.

Warning! Six or more of these symptoms and you may be at risk of excellent health.

The Greek philosopher Socrates was famous for teaching people 'Know thyself.' It is told that one of his students asked him whether he actually followed his own advice. Did he know himself? Socrates replied, 'No, but I understand something about this not knowing.'

Glossary of NLP Terms

Accessing Cues	The ways we tune our bodies by breathing, posture, gesture and eye movements to think in certain ways.
Anchor	Any stimulus that evokes a response. Anchors change our *state*. They can occur naturally or be set up intentionally.
Anchoring	The process of associating one thing with another.
Associated State	Inside an experience, seeing through your own eyes, fully in your senses.
Auditory	To do with the sense of hearing.
Baseline State	That *state* of mind which is normal and habitual.
Behaviour	Any activity that we engage in, including thought processes; one of the *neurological levels*.
Beliefs	The *generalizations* we make about ourselves, others and the world, and our operating principles in it; one of the *neurological levels*.
Beyond Identity	That level of experience where you are most yourself and most your Self and you are most connected with others, the spiritual level; one of the *neurological levels*.
Body Language	The way we communicate with our bodies, without words or sounds, for example our posture, gestures, facial expressions, appearance and *accessing cues*.
Break State	Using movement or distraction to change an emotional *state*.

Calibration	Accurately recognizing another person's state by reading non-verbal signals.
Capability	A successful *strategy* for carrying out a task. A skill or habit. Also a habitual way of thinking. One of the *neurological levels*.
Congruence	Alignment of *beliefs*, *values*, skills and action. Being in rapport with yourself.
Conscious	Anything in present moment awareness.
Deletion	Missing out a portion of an experience.
Dissociated State	Being at one remove from an experience, seeing or hearing it from the outside.
Distortion	Changing experience, making it different in some way.
Emotional State	See *State*.
Environment	The where, the when and the people we are with; one of the *neurological levels*.
Eye Accessing Cues	Movements of the eyes in certain directions which indicate visual, *auditory* or *kinesthetic* thinking.
First Position	Perceiving the world from your own point of view only. Being in touch with your own inner reality. One of three different perceptual positions, the others being *second* and *third position*.
Flexibility	Having many choices of thought and behaviour to achieve an *outcome*. One of the four pillars of NLP.
Generalization	The process by which one specific experience comes to represent a whole class of experiences.
Gustatory	To do with the sense of taste.
Identity	Your self-image or self-concept, who you take yourself to be; one of the *neurological levels*.
In Time	Having a *timeline* where the past is behind you and the future in front, with the 'now' part passing through your body.
Incongruence	*State* of being out of *rapport* with yourself, having internal conflict expressed in *behaviour*. It may be sequential – for example, one action followed by another

	that contradicts it – or simultaneous – for example, agreement in words but with a doubtful voice tone.
Internal Dialogue	Self talk.
Kinesthetic	The feeling sense, tactile sensations and internal feelings such as remembered sensations, emotions and the sense of balance.
Leading	Changing what you do with enough *rapport* for the other person to follow.
Logical Levels	See *Neurological Levels*.
Map of Reality	Each person's unique representation of the world built from their individual perceptions and experiences.
Matching	Adopting parts of another person's *behaviour*, skills, *beliefs* or *values* for the purpose of enhancing *rapport*.
Meta Model	A set of language patterns and questions that link language with experience.
Metaphor	Indirect communication by a story or figure of speech implying a comparison. In NLP metaphor covers similes, stories, parables and allegories.
Modal Operators	A linguistic term for words that imply rules such as 'should', 'must', 'can' and 'cannot'.
Modelling	The process of discerning the sequence of ideas and *behaviour* that enables someone to accomplish a task. The basis of NLP.
MULTIPLE DESCRIPTION	The wisdom of having different points of view of the same event. There are three perceptual positions: *first position* is your own reality; *second position* is another person's reality; and *third position* is a detached viewpoint. Having all three is called a *triple description*.
Neuro-Linguistic Programming	The study of excellence and the study of the structure of subjective experience.
Neurological Levels	Different levels of experience: *environment, behaviour, capability, beliefs, identity* and *beyond identity*.

Nominalization	Linguistic term for the process of turning a verb into an abstract noun; also the word for the noun so formed. For example, 'relating' becomes 'the relationship': a process has become a thing.
Olfactory	To do with the sense of smell.
Outcome	A specific, sensory-based, desired goal. You know what you will see, hear and feel when you have it. One of the four pillars of NLP.
Pacing	Gaining and maintaining *rapport* with another person over a period of time by meeting them in their *map of reality*. Pacing yourself is paying attention to your own experience without immediately trying to change it.
Positive Intention	The positive purpose underlying any action or *belief*.
Preferred Representational System	The *representational system* that an individual typically uses most to think consciously and organize their experience.
Presuppositions	Ideas or *beliefs* that are presupposed, i.e. taken for granted and acted upon.
Rapport	A relationship of trust and responsiveness with self or others. One of the four pillars of NLP.
Reframing	Seeing an experience from another point of view, giving it a different meaning.
Representational System	The different channels whereby we re-present information on the inside, using our senses: visual (sight), *auditory* (hearing), *kinesthetic* (body sensation), *olfactory* (smell) and *gustatory* (taste).
Resources	Anything that can help achieve an *outcome*, e.g. physiology, *states*, thoughts, *beliefs*, *strategies*, experiences, people, events, possessions, places, stories, etc.
Second Position	Experiencing the point of view of another person.
Self-Modelling	*Modelling* your own *states* of excellence as *resources*.
Sensory Acuity	The process of learning to make finer and

more useful distinctions from the sensory information we get from the world. One of the four pillars of NLP.

Somatic Pacing	Paying attention to your own body experience.
State	The sum of our thoughts, feelings, emotions, physical and mental energy.
Strategy	A repeatable sequence of thought and *behaviour* which consistently produces a particular *outcome*.
Submodalities	The fine distinctions we make within each *representational system*, the qualities of our internal representations, the smallest building blocks of our thoughts.
Third Position	Taking the viewpoint of a detached observer, the systemic view.
Through Time	Having a *timeline* where past, present and future are all in front of you.
Timeline	The line that connects your past with your future; the way we store pictures, sounds and feelings of our past, present and future.
Triple Description	Seeing an event from *first*, *second* and *third position*.
Unconscious	Everything that is not in your present moment awareness.
Values	Those things, like health, that are important to you.

GLOSSARY OF MEDICAL TERMS

ACTH
(adrenocorti-
cotrophin)

A *hormone* secreted by the *pituitary gland.*
It stimulates the *adrenal gland* to produce
cortisol.

Active Placebo

A drug with a definite physiological effect
that does not directly affect the *illness* for
which it is prescribed.

Acute

Sudden onset of symptoms or pain that
lasts for a short while.

Adrenal Glands

Endocrine glands located one above each
kidney. The outer part (the cortex)
produces steroid *hormones* under the
control of *ACTH.* The inner part (the
medulla) produces the *hormones*
adrenaline (epinephrine) and *noradrenaline*
(norepinephrine).

Adrenaline
(epinephrine)

A *hormone* produced by the adrenal
medulla. Its release is stimulated by the
sympathetic nervous system to prepare the
body for action.

Adrenocorti-
cotrophin

See *ACTH.*

Allergen

A substance capable of producing an *allergy*
in a susceptible person, e.g. chocolate,
house dust, wasp venom, pollen.

Allergy

Hypersensitive state of the *immune system*
caused by a reaction to *allergens* in the
environment.

Allopathic medicine

Term used to describe modern medicine
covering all methods of treating *disease.*

Analgesic

Pain-relieving drug.

Anatomy

The study of the structure of the body.

Antibody	A protein produced by the *immune system* to render specific *antigens* harmless.
Antibiotics	A class of powerful antibacterial drugs.
Anticoagulant	Chemical that prevents the blood from clotting, e.g. heparin.
Antigen	Any substance or organism that stimulates the *immune system* to produce *antibodies.*
Asthma	An allergic condition where the body reacts by constricting the breathing tubes of the lungs leading to respiratory problems. Severe asthma attacks can be fatal.
Attributional Style	Way of explaining events using deletion, distortion and generalization to give optimistic or pessimistic explanations of events.
Autoimmune Disease	Condition that is caused by the *immune system* reacting against an *antigen* that is part of the body itself. For example, *rheumatoid arthritis.*
Autonomic Nervous System	That part of the nervous system that regulates certain unconscious processes such as the heart rate and digestion. It has two branches: the sympathetic, which activates, and the parasympathetic, which relaxes.
Bacteria	Micro-organisms consisting of one cell, ubiquitous in the environment. May cause *disease* in susceptible hosts.
B-Cells	*Immune system* cells that multiply and produce *antibodies* designed to neutralize specific *antigens.*
Blood Pressure	Force exerted by the blood against the walls of the arteries.
Cancer	Malignant tumour consisting of abnormal body cells with no normal limits to their growth.
Carcinogen	Substance with the potential of causing *cancer.*
Cell Mediated Immunity	One of the two methods the *immune system* has to defend the body by using specialized

cells to dispose of tumours, parasites and *viruses* that are recognized as not being part of the body.

Central Nervous System	The brain and spinal cord.
Cholesterol	Fatty substance formed in the body. Excessive amounts in the blood are associated with an increased risk of heart *disease*.
Chronic	Long lasting or recurrent.
Cortisol	Powerful adrenal *hormone* released in the *stress* response. Alters muscle tone, increases secretion of stomach acids, and has an anti-inflammatory and immuno-suppressive effect.
Corticotrophin- Releasing Factor (CRF)	*Hormone* secreted by the *hypothalamus* that regulates the release of *ACTH* by the *pituitary gland*.
CRF	See *Corticotrophin-Releasing Factor*.
Diabetes	A disorder of the carbohydrate *metabolism* resulting in excessive amounts of sugar in the blood. May arise as an *autoimmune disease*.
Diagnosis	Identification of *disease* or *illness* from the symptoms.
Disease	Demonstrable pathological process which may affect the whole body or any of its parts.
Double Blind Trial	Procedure used to test the effectiveness of a drug against an inert preparation (*placebo*). Neither the patients nor the dispensing doctor know who receives the placebo and who receives the drug.
Endocrine Glands	System of glands in the body that secrete *hormones*, directed by the *pituitary gland*.
Endorphin	A natural pain reliever made by the body.
Enkephalin	A natural pain reliever produced by the body.
Epinephrine	See *Adrenaline*.
Free Radicals	Reactive molecules produced naturally in

the body that have the potential to damage cells.

Health
Natural state of balance and well-being in the mind, body and spirit.

Histamine
Substance secreted by the *mast cells*. It dilates capillaries and constricts muscles in the lungs. Plays an important part in allergic reactions.

Holistic Medicine
An approach that aims to treat the patient as a whole person and not just the symptoms of *disease* in their body.

Homoeopathic Medicine
System of medicine that treats the whole person. It treats the symptom with very weak preparations of substances that can produce the same or similar symptoms.

Hormone
Chemical messenger produced by an *endocrine gland* that has far-reaching effects on the body, for example testosterone and insulin.

Humoral Immunity
Immunity acquired from being exposed to *antigens* so that *antibodies* are produced.

Hypertension
High blood pressure.

Hypothalamus
A small portion of the forebrain. It is closely associated with the *autonomic nervous system* and endocrine system. It also regulates many unconscious bodily activities such as hunger and temperature.

Iatrogenic Illness
Condition caused by medical treatment.

Illness
Subjective feeling of ill-*health*; may be caused by a *disease*.

Immune System
That part of our physiology that protects our physiological identity by dealing with *antigens*.

Immunoglobulin
Complex chains of protein on the surface of *immune system* cells.

Immunology
Study of the *immune system*.

Inflammation
Swelling of tissue, one of the body's reactions to injury, regulated by the *immune system*.

Learned Helplessness
The theory that people can be conditioned into a state of helplessness, believing

nothing they do will make a difference.
First put forward by Martin Seligman.

Leukocytes	White blood cells of the *immune system*.
Limbic System	Part of the mid brain mainly associated with emotional expression.
Lymphatic System	Circulatory system for *immune system* cells. Lymph fluid collects in the several lymph nodes throughout the body.
Lymphocytes	*Immune system* cells produced and carried mainly in the *lymphatic system*.
Macrophages	*Immune system* cells that engulf cell debris.
Mast Cells	*Immune system* cells that release heparin, *serotonin* and *histamine*, substances which regulate *inflammation*.
Metabolism	The working processes of the body that produce energy.
Morphine	Strong pain-relieving drug.
Neurology	Study of the nervous system.
Neuropeptide	*Neurotransmitter* made up of amino acids.
Neurotransmitters	Chemicals produced at nerve endings, bringing about bodily change. They are the main means whereby nerves communicate with each other.
Neutrophils	*Immune system* cells that engulf *bacteria*.
NK (Natural Killer) Cells	Cells of the *immune system* that destroy *cancer* cells and cells infected by *viruses*.
Nocebo	Type of *placebo* that gives undesired effects such as nausea, allergic reactions and addictions.
Noradrenaline (norepinephrine)	*Hormone* acting as a *neurotransmitter* formed by the *sympathetic nervous system* nerve endings.
Norepinephrine	See *Noradrenaline*.
Osteoporosis	Progressive reduction in bone density making the skeleton more brittle.
Parasympathetic Nervous System	The branch of the *autonomic nervous system* that has a relaxing affect on many unconscious processes such as heart rate and digestion.
Pathogens	Agents such as *bacteria* and *viruses* that produce *disease*.

Pathology	The study of *disease.*
Phagocyte	*Immune system* cells that destroy *antigens* by engulfing them.
Physiology	Study of how the body functions or a description of the bodily aspects of the person.
Pituitary Gland	Small gland at the base of the brain attached to the *hypothalamus.* Master gland of the endocrine system, secreting *hormones* that affect other *endocrine glands.*
Placebo	An inert substance or treatment that does not have a direct effect on the *illness,* yet may heal or cure the condition because it mobilizes the patient's natural healing powers.
PNI	See *Psychoneuroimmunology.*
Prognosis	Prediction of the course of the *disease.*
Psycho-neuroimmunology (PNI)	Branch of medicine that studies the relationship between the mind, the nervous system and the *immune system.*
Rheumatoid Arthritis	A *chronic autoimmune disease* where the *immune system* attacks connective tissue in the joints causing *inflammation.*
Serotonin	An important *neurotransmitter* that regulates rest and sleep.
Stress	The flight or fight response that activates the *sympathetic nervous system* and results in the release of many *hormones* and *neurotransmitters. Chronic stress* damages the body and can result in high *blood pressure,* digestive troubles, sleep disorders, headaches and accelerated ageing.
Stressor	Experience that results in *stress.*
Sympathetic Nervous System	Branch of the *autonomic nervous system* that energizes many unconscious processes such as digestion and heart rate.
T-Cells	*Immune system* cells made in the bone marrow and stored in the *thymus* gland. 'Killer' T-cells destroy *cancer* cells and virally infected cells. 'Helper' T-cells signal to the immune system that action is needed.

	'Suppressor' T-cells stop the action when it is over.
Thymus	A small gland located under the breastbone. It stores the *immune system T-cells*.
Tryptophan	Amino acid needed to make *serotonin*.
Ultradian Rhythms	Natural rhythms of rest and activity and hemispheric dominance that occur within a day.
Virus	A minute infectious agent that can only grow and reproduce inside living cells. Viruses invade the cell and take over its functions to produce more viruses.
Warts	Harmless skin growths caused by a *virus*.

BIBLIOGRAPHY

This is a personal selection of books that we have found interesting and useful in the field of health generally.

Andreas, Connirae and Steve, *Heart of the Mind*, Real People Press, 1990

Benson, Herbert, *The Relaxation Response*, Avon, 1975

Borysenko, Joan, *Minding the Body, Mending the Mind*, Addison-Wesley Books, 1987

Brahe, Carl, *Healing on the Edge of Now*, Sunshine Press, 1992

Chopra, Deepak, *Quantum Healing*, Bantam, 1989

—, *Ageless Body, Timeless Mind*, Rider, 1993

Cousins, Norman, *Head First*, Penguin, 1990

Dilts, Robert, Hallbom, Tim, and Smith, Suzi, *Beliefs: Pathways to health and well-being*, Metamorphous Press, 1990

Dossey, Larry, *Medicine and Meaning*, Bantam, 1991

Elgin, Suzette Hayden, *Staying Well with the Gentle Art of Verbal Self-Defence*, Prentice Hall, 1990

Foss, Laurence, and Rothenberg, Kenneth, *The Second Medical Revolution*, Shambhala, 1988

Hirshberg, Caryle, and Barasch, Marc, *Remarkable Recovery*, Riverhead Books, 1995

Justice, Blair, *Who Gets Sick*, Tarcher, 1987

Kabat-Zinn, Jon, *Full Catastrophe Living*, Delta, 1990

King, Mark, Novik, Larry, and Citrenbaum, Charles, *Irresistible Communication: Creative skills for the health professional*, W. B. Saunders, 1983

Kübler-Ross, Elizabeth, *On Death and Dying*, Tavistock, 1969

Kuhn, Thomas, *The Structure of Scientific Revolutions*, University of Chicago Press, 1982

Le Han, Lawrence, *Cancer as a Turning Point*, Plume, 1990

Locke, Steven, and Colligan, Douglas, *The Healer Within*, Mentor Books, 1986

O'Connor, Joseph, and Seymour, John, *Introducing NLP*, Thorsons, 1990

O'Connor, Joseph, and McDermott, Ian, *Principles of NLP*, Thorsons, 1996

Nuland, Sherwin, *How We Die*, Chatto & Windus, 1993

Ornstein, Robert, and Sobel, David, *The Healing Brain*, Simon and Schuster, 1987

—, *Healthy Pleasures*, Addison-Wesley, 1989

Pearson, Dirk, and Shaw, Sandy, *Life Extension*, Warner, 1983

Pelletier, Kenneth, *Mind as Healer, Mind as Slayer*, Delta, 1977

Peterson, Christopher, and Bossio, Lisa, *Health and Optimism*, The Free Press, 1991

Rossi, Ernest, *The Psychobiology of Mind Body Healing*, W. W. Norton, 1986

Rushworth, Claire, *Making a Difference in Cancer Care*, Souvenir Press, 1994

Selye, Hans, *The Stress of Life*, McGraw-Hill, 1976

Siegel Bernie, *Love, Medicine and Miracles*, Harper and Row, 1986

Simonton, O. Carl and Stephanie, *Getting Well Again*, Bantam, 1992

Skrabanek, Petr, and McCormick, James, *Follies and Fallacies in Medicine*, Tarragon Press, 1994

Wallace, Robert, *The Neurophysiology of Enlightenment*, Maharishi International University Press, 1991

Neil, Andrew, *Health and Healing*, Houghton-Mifflin, 1983

NLP AND HEALTH RESOURCES

The following organizations host the NLP and health certification training:

Brazil
Synapsis
R Paes de Aranjo
29/96 Sao Paulo
Telephone International +55 011 822 8181

Denmark
NLP Dansk
Sankelmarksdej 23–25
8600 Silkeborg
Telephone International +45 86 80 1911

England
International Teaching Seminars
7 Rudall Crescent
London NW3 1RS
Telephone International +44 181 442 4133

Germany
Milton H. Erikson Institute
Wartburgstrasse 17
D–10825 Berlin
Telephone International +49 30 781 7795

Mexico
PNL Mexico
Lerdo de Tejada
2485C
44130 Guadalajara
Jal.
Telephone International +52 36 15 8447

USA
Institute for the Advanced Studies of Health
Anchor Point Associates
346 South
500 East
Salt Lake City
Utah 84102
Telephone International +1 801 534 1022

Dynamic Learning Centre
PO Box 1112
Ben Lomond
95005 California
Telephone International +1 408 336 3457

TRAINING AND RESOURCES

There is a growing number of individuals and organizations who want to use NLP in their training and development. NLP training is a significant investment that can give substantial benefits in increased skills and well-being. It is important to have excellent training from the start. NLP is experiential. We suggest you go for high quality training which means that you leave the course being able to do NLP and not just talk about it.

International Teaching Seminars has pioneered hands on, skill-based NLP training with practical applications. Software and tapes are also available.

For details of the following trainings, software and tapes contact:

International Teaching Seminars (ITS)
7 Rudall Crescent
London NW3 1RS

Tel: International +44 181 442 4133
Fax: International +44 181 442 4155
Internet: World Wide Web site http://www.nlp-community.com

ITS Training

Open evenings that focus on practical applications of NLP.
NLP and Health Training
A two or three-day training open to all. Also offered as in-house training.

NLP Health Certification Training
An advanced 20-day certification programme taken over nine months.

NLP: First Principles
A three-day introduction to NLP and how to use it immediately. Based on the book *Principles of NLP* by Joseph O'Connor and Ian McDermott (Thorsons, 1996).

NLP Practitioner Training
A comprehensive programme with a focus on the practical applications of NLP, leading to a fully recognized practitioner certification. No previous training is required.

NLP Master Practitioner Training
A complete and fully recognized certification programme with a team of international NLP trainers.

Professional Development Program

Training in how to use NLP to become an effective leader, present yourself and your ideas powerfully, and manage relationships.

NLP Audiocassettes

Deep Trance Relaxation
An easy and effortless relaxation process (single tape).

What is NLP?
A set of guiding principles, knowledge and skills – a systematic means of achieving consistently outstanding results (single tape).

Professional Development Program
A complete programme of how to use NLP to be an effective leader, to manage work and personal relationships and to present yourself and your ideas supremely well (six tape set).

Tools for Transformation
How to build choice, change perspective and make sense of behaviour through reframing and to use submodalities for easy change. Recorded at the ITS NLP practitioner training (four tape set).

Freedom from the Past
Live demonstrations, commentary and explanation of the NLP
phobia cure and profound trauma resolution (two tapes).

Modelling Projects

Identifying and modelling examples of excellence in various fields
to discover what it is that makes them excel and designing training
to pass on these patterns to others.

ITS Consultancy

The professional application of NLP to the practical needs of
large- and small-scale organizations.

NLP Software

NLP Personal Development Software: Goal Wizard
The first in a suite of windows-based programs that do not
require previous NLP training. It enables you to keep track of
individual, team and organizational outcomes, store them by category, examine the relationships between them and clarify them
so they are realistic, motivating and achievable. It is suitable for
personal or business outcomes and ideal for clarifying your
health goals.
All software works on any IBM compatible PC with Windows 3.1.

For further details contact ITS Software: International +44 181
442 4133

Psychological Software Development

Joseph O'Connor and Ian McDermott are experienced in designing software to train NLP and communication skills in a way that
uses the medium to its fullest capability.

Credits

We have done our best to track down and credit the sources of the
material in this book. Please let us know by mail if we have inad-
vertently omitted an important source or if you feel someone is

not properly acknowledged. We will do our best to correct future printings.

Feedback

If you found this book valuable and would like to tell us why, or you have responses or suggestions, we would like to hear from you. We would also be very interested in examples of how using NLP has influenced your health. Please write to us at International Teaching Seminars.

ABOUT THE AUTHORS

Joseph O'Connor

Joseph O'Connor is a leading author, trainer and consultant in the field of NLP, communications skills and systems thinking. He is a certified trainer of NLP. He became interested in NLP in the mid 1980s as it brought together a number of themes that have fascinated him for many years – how we create our experience, and what distinguishes the ordinary from the exceptional, especially in the field of the performing arts. Joseph uses NLP in many ways, training and consulting in business, modelling fine athletic performance, and working with athletes on mental training. He sees many ideas from artistic and sports mental training as being relevant to business coaching and consulting.

As a trained musician and guitarist, his involvement in the arts has led to modelling projects in theatre and musical performance. He has always been interested in health, how mind and body help or hinder people in their search for health and happiness, and to be able to write about those discoveries and experiences has been delightful.

Other books:
Not Pulling Strings, Lambent Books, 1987
Introducing NLP (with John Seymour), Thorsons, 1990
Training with NLP (with John Seymour), Thorsons, 1994
Successful Selling with NLP (with Robin Prior), Thorsons, 1995
Mind Power (contributing author)
   – *Developing your leadership qualities*, Timelife, 1995
   – *Take control of your life*, Timelife, 1996
Practical NLP for Managers (with Ian McDermott), Gower, 1996
Principles of NLP (with Ian McDermott), Thorsons, 1996
The Art of Systems Thinking (with Ian McDermott)

Contact Joseph at:
c/o Lambent Books
4 Coombe Gardens
New Malden
Surrey KT3 4AA

Telephone: +44 (0) 181 715 2560
Fax: +44 (0) 181 715 2560
E-Mail: lambent@well.com
Internet: http://www.lambent.com

Ian McDermott

Ian McDermott is a Certified NLP Trainer and an International NLP Diplomate. Ian first became interested in NLP in the early 1980s. He was attracted to NLP because it offered both a unifying model of successful change work and practical tools for achieving results.

As a trainer he was fascinated by the means NLP used to achieve this – namely looking at what people actually do and unpacking what works so that it can be taught to others.

He has had a lifelong interest in the way we use our thinking to help or hinder us achieve our desires. It has caused him to research different techniques for harnessing the power of the mind, including meditation. Noticing the benefits, he has meditated regularly since 1977.

It also meant that he became especially interested in the relation between the mind and body and how this could affect one's health. He has worked with many people who have had health issues. More recently in collaboration with Robert Dilts, Tim Hallbom and Suzi Smith, he has been training and establishing a core of NLP health specialists in the UK. He also frequently runs NLP and health trainings open to all.

Ian is Director of Training for International Teaching Seminars.

Other books (with Joseph O'Connor):
MindPower (contributing author)
   – *Developing your leadership qualities*, Timelife, 1995
   – *Take control of your life*, Timelife, 1996
Practical NLP for Managers, Gower, 1996

Principles of NLP, Thorsons, 1996

Contact Ian at:
International Teaching Seminars
7 Rudall Crescent
London NW3 1RS
England

Telephone +44 (0)181 442 4133
Fax +44 (0)181 442 4155
Internet http://www.nlp–community.com